T0381112

OTHER BOOKS BY

PEGGY RICHERSON YANCY

Then Let It Spill
Dearly Beloved
Love And Marriage
In The Presence Of His Peace

IN OTHER WORDS . . .

Contemplation of God's Holy Word

Using The
King James Version (KJV) and
New King James Version (NKJV)

PEGGY RICHERSON YANCY

WESTBOW
PRESS®
A DIVISION OF THOMAS NELSON
& ZONDERVAN

Scripture taken from the King James Version of the Bible.

Scripture taken from the New King James Version®. Copyright © 1982 by Thomas Nelson. Used by permission. All rights reserved.

WestBow Press books may be ordered through booksellers or by contacting:

WestBow Press
A Division of Thomas Nelson & Zondervan
1663 Liberty Drive
Bloomington, IN 47403
www.westbowpress.com
1 (866) 928-1240

ISBN: 978-1-9736-2725-8 (sc)
ISBN: 978-1-9736-2626-8 (e)

Library of Congress Control Number: 2018905158

Print information available on the last page.

WestBow Press rev. date: 04/26/2018

DEDICATED TO

My beloved children: Keith, Kevin, Patia, David,
and each of their precious progeny.

INTRODUCTION

How changeable are the seasons! We go through Springtime, Summer, Fall, and Winter trying to cope with the temperature changes and pollen dispersions that each season brings. The varying seasons of our lives are filled with many other challenges, making us wish for a newscaster to predict what could be coming next. Life is a complex situation that confounds us over and again. We need a book of directions when we wonder, "What now?"

As an eighty nine year old widow and grandmother, looking back on the changing seasons of my life, I realize that the desired book of directions was always available, but often overlooked. I see clearly now, in this mature season of my life, that the Holy Bible holds all that we need to know about living this earthly life. As a child I discovered truths that were often beyond my full comprehension. Thankfully, my beloved parents introduced me as a toddler to the promises of God found within His inspired Holy Word. This blessing has proved to be a treasure beyond measure throughout my lifetime.

"IN OTHER WORDS..." brings God's promises alive with depth and understanding for every season of life. May God bless all who contemplate His Holy Word, that our lives may be transformed by His grace.

JANUARY 1

Ask, and it shall be given you; seek, and ye shall find; knock, and it shall be opened unto you.
—Matthew 7:7 (KJV)

In Other Words...

God knows our situation, whatever it may be. He will be our helper, but He waits to be invited into our lives. God is not intrusive. He desires fellowship with all His creation, and we need His companionship! Talk to Him about your needs; keep your eyes and ears open to His Spirit's leading. He will make a way for you!

JANUARY 2

For all have sinned, and come
short of the glory of God.
—Romans 3:23 (KJV)

In Other Words…

We try to run with all our strength, but time and
again we stumble and fall. Only Jesus ran the perfect
race throughout His life on earth, without sin at
any time along the way. He gave us an example
for every life situation; full of grace and truth.

JANUARY 3

A merry heart does good, like a medicine.
—Proverbs 17:22 (NKJV)

In Other Words...

Give me a smile, Lord, one deep from
inside, down where the giggles and belly
laughs hide. Give me a smile Lord,
just let one sneak out; unbuckle a
chuckle when gloom lurks about!

JANUARY 4

For by grace you have been saved through
faith, and that not of yourselves; it is
the gift of God, not of works,
lest anyone should boast.
—Ephesians 2:8-9 (NKJV)

In Other Words…

We have been given a free and undeserved
gift! All we have to do is accept it! Be thankful
for the blessed gift of faith! It is a treasure
beyond measure, paid for at great cost
by Jesus Christ!

JANUARY 5

The Lord is my shepherd; I shall not want.
—Psalm 23:1 (KJV)

In Other Words...

The Bible often compares God's children to sheep.
If sheep stumble to the ground, they can't get back
onto their feet without help. Sheep don't have claws
or sharp teeth for protection; they are defenseless.
Without the shepherd's watchful care, they would
live in constant danger. We have problems, too!
Thankfully God understands our every need, and
He cares for us! He is our good shepherd keeping
us safe and at peace within His watchful care.

JANUARY 6

Delight yourself also in the Lord; and He
shall give you the desires of your heart.
—Psalm 37:4 (NKJV)

In Other Words…

How can we say thanks for all God's goodness?
We are so small and He is so great! May we
choose to live in ways that are acceptable in
His sight that our hearts may become filled
to overflowing with abundant life!

JANUARY 7

Christ in you, the hope of glory.
—Colossians 1:27 (KJV)

In Other Words...

When we allow Jesus to be at home in our
hearts, miraculous changes come about.
He can transform our puny actions and
aspirations into His glorious plans for
abundant living eternally!

JANUARY 8

Create in me a clean heart, O God; and
renew a right spirit within me.
—Psalm 51:10 (KJV)

In Other Words...

Remodel me, please God. Replace my
frazzled ways with refreshing, durable
designs of your miraculous creation.

JANUARY 9

Do not be conformed to this world, but be
transformed by the renewing of your mind,
that you may prove what is that good and
acceptable and perfect will of God.
—Romans 12:2 (NKJV)

In Other Words...

Don't copy popular fickle fads! Chasing after the
lifestyle designs of this world is not what God
fashioned for His children! Follow His directions
carefully, taking note of each detail He has lovingly
planned. May we become completely refreshed;
changed into a model of His righteousness!

JANUARY 10

In every thing by prayer and supplication
with thanksgiving let your requests
be made known unto God.
—Philippians 4:6 (KJV)

In Other Words...

O God, Your loving promises fill me with joy
and thankfulness! Humbly, I pray for the ability
to comprehend Your awesome foreknowledge
of all things, and Your predestination for each
human being. Your grace will be sufficient for
me, until the day of full understanding comes.

JANUARY 11

The law of the Lord is perfect, converting
the soul; the testimony of the Lord is sure,
making wise the simple. The statutes of
the Lord are right, rejoicing the heart.
—Psalm 19:7-8 (KJV)

In Other Words...

All we need to understand is provided
through the law of the Lord, which is clearly
given for our comprehension. Only
obedience to God's directions
leads us to abundant joy.

JANUARY 12

God is our refuge and strength, a very present help
in trouble.
—Psalm 46:1 (KJV)

In Other Words…

When the storms of life are
overwhelming, we can feel
secure within God's loving promises.
He is with us always!

JANUARY 13

Go therefore and make disciples of all nations,
baptizing them in the name of the Father, and
of the Son, and of the Holy Spirit, teaching them
to observe all things that I have commanded
you; and, lo, I am with you always,
even unto the end of the age.
—Matthew 28:19-20 (NKJV)

In Other Words...

Ready, set, "Go!" was Jesus' final command
to His followers. Tell the good news of
God's love to everyone everywhere! His
Holy Spirit will always go beside us!

JANUARY 14

But God demonstrates His own love toward us, in that while we were still sinners, Christ died for us.
—Romans 5:8 (NKJV)

In Other Words…

Such love beyond measure! Jesus left the glories of heaven and came down to earth to make a way for us to be forgiven of our sins! By faith in His life, death, and resurrection, God's children may repent and be covered by His sacrificial blood to find forgiveness and receive the gift of grace and mercy for eternity!

JANUARY 15

And God will wipe away all tears from their eyes; and there shall be no more death, neither sorrow, nor crying, neither shall there be any more pain; for the former things are passed away.
—Revelation 21:4 (KJV)

In Other Words...

O, the bliss of eternal springtime! For each of God's children there will be a heavenly spring-cleaning time! God will wipe away all the tears that have accumulated; He will remove the dust of death and sadness! We will be welcomed home at last, and lovingly received by our Savior! The clutter of our earthly life will be over and done; eternity's new day has begun! Praise God now and forever!

JANUARY 16

For what shall it profit a man, if he shall gain the whole world, and lose his own soul?
—Mark 8:36 (KJV)

In Other Words…

Oh, how we enjoy collecting things! This, that, or the other; some new, some old. Our lives become crowded, overflowing with prized possessions. Space is needed! We must make room, a treasured place within our heart, to protect the one possession of greatest value… our own soul!

JANUARY 17

He hath shown you, O man, what is good; and what
does the Lord require of you, but to do justly, to
love mercy, and to walk humbly with your God?
—Micah 6:8 (NKJV)

In Other Words…

The inspired word of God clearly reveals how to truly
honor God. We must humbly obey Him; be fair to
one and all, be forgiving, and arrogant never, ever.

JANUARY 18

Peace I leave with you, my peace I give
unto you; not as the world giveth do I
give unto you. Let not your heart be
troubled, neither let it be afraid.
—John 14:27 (KJV)

In Other Words…

What a relief to be told: "At ease!" from the One in
control. Obey and be blessed, freed from turmoil and
strife! Enjoy the sweet gift of peace that God gives. O,
the beauty of the calm and stillness that God gives
to his children; peace of heart and mind and soul!

JANUARY 19

Bless the Lord, O my soul; and all that is within
me, bless His holy name! Bless the Lord, O
my soul, and forget not all His benefits.
—Psalm 103:1-3 (KJV)

In Other Words...

How can we begin to remember all Your benefits,
Lord? We are covered by your goodness: the very air
we breathe, the energizing sunlight, and soothing
darkness, abundant nourishment, and the delight of
loved ones, the strength for every good purpose that
You inspire! Your kindness and grace are heaped
upon us day after day! May our truly thankful hearts
be a blessing to You in return, we humbly pray.

JANUARY 20

I am the way, the truth, and the
life. No one comes to the
Father except through me.
—John 14:6 (NKJV)

In Other Words...

Jesus spoke those words very clearly: "I AM..."
Moses heard those words from God, too, when
He spoke to him from a burning bush: "I AM..."
Directions were given for deliverance from slavery!
Blessed Trinity of God the Father, God the Son, and
God the Holy Spirit, nudging us to grasp the wonder
of the way, the truth, and of the life of the great I AM!

JANUARY 21

I am the light of the world; He who follows Me shall
not walk in darkness, but have the light of life.
—John 8:12 (NKJV)

In Other Words…

The splendor of God's glory brightens all
of creation! No more stumbling through
the darkness; for now we are able to see the
footsteps of Jesus, and we can follow on!

JANUARY 22

If God be for us, who can be against us?
—Romans 8:31 (KJV)

In Other Words...

Let's determine to be on God's
side! He will always win!

JANUARY 23

I beseech you therefore, brethren, by the
mercies of God, that ye present your bodies
a living sacrifice, holy, acceptable unto
God, which is your reasonable service.
—Romans 12:1 (KJV)

In Other Words…

Considering all that God has done for us, we are
only asked to be available to Him…wherever that
may lead us…for our good and for His glory.

JANUARY 24

Jesus Christ the same yesterday,
and today, and forever.
—Hebrews 13:8 (KJV)

In Other Words...

Our Savior never changes. He was, He is, He shall
always be the loving guide to mercy and forgiveness
for everyone of days past, present, and future!

JANUARY 25

Let not your heart be troubled; ye believe in God,
believe also in me. In my Father's house are many
mansions; if it were not so, I would have told you. I
go to prepare a place for you. And if I go and prepare
a place for you, I will come again, and receive you
unto myself; that where I am, there ye may be also.
—John 14:1-3 (KJV)

In Other Words...

May our hearts simply trust in Jesus' words
of love! We shall be welcomed by Him
one wonderful day when He comes for us!
O, glorious Homecoming Day in heaven!

JANUARY 26

Nor height, nor depth, nor any other created creature shall be able to separate us from the love of God, which is in Christ Jesus our Lord.
—Romans 8:39 (KJV)

In Other Words…

Whether we journey up into outer space, or down into the deepest sea, or find ourselves bereft by the myriad complexities of life, our loving Lord will stay beside us all the way!

JANUARY 27

In everything give thanks; for this is the
will of God in Christ Jesus for you.
—1 Thessalonians 5:18 (NKJV)

In Other Words...

Whatever the situation, whether good or
bad, there is always much for which to
be thankful. The Lord is with us,
working things out!

JANUARY 28

Open thou mine eyes, that I may see
wondrous things from Your law.
—Psalm 119:18 (NKJV)

In Other Words…

The Ten Commandments provide God's
directions to the way of right living that is
pleasing in His sight, and to others. Obeying
His law always works for our good!

JANUARY 29

Put on the whole armor of God, that ye may be able to stand against the wiles of the devil.
—Ephesian 6:11 (KJV)

In Other Words...

Piece by piece, word for word, may we choose to place God's Holy Word within our heart and mind, to sustain and protect our thoughts and actions from all enticing deceitfulness, which ultimately will lead to destruction.

JANUARY 30

Restore unto me the joy of thy salvation.
—Psalm 51:12 (KJV)

In Other Words…

Come back again, I pray. Fill my heart to
overflowing with the delight of Your love
for me; Your grace, Your mercy, O Lord.

JANUARY 31

There is therefore now no condemnation
to those who are in Christ Jesus…
—Romans 8:1 (NKJV)

In Other Words…

What wonderful words of GOOD NEWS! By faith
in our redeemer Christ Jesus, we believers are
covered by His blood and forgiven eternally!

FEBRUARY 1

Sing unto the Lord, bless His name; proclaim the
good news of His salvation from day to day.
—Psalm 96:2 (NKJV)

In Other Words…

O, the beauty of the melody that we
thankfully lift in celebration of God's love
for us, croaking as our voices may be!

FEBRUARY 2

The Spirit Himself bears witness with our spirit that
we are the children of God, and if children, then
heirs...heirs of God and joint heirs with Christ.
—Romans 8:16-17 (NKJV)

In Other Words...

By faith we become adopted sons
and daughters of God!
O, the glory of that loving affirmation!

FEBRUARY 3

The Lord gave, and the Lord hath taken
away; blessed be the name of the Lord.
—Job 1:21 (KJV)

In Other Words…

We who live by faith realize that we are in
God's hands, from beginning to end.

FEBRUARY 4

But they that wait upon the Lord shall renew
their strength; they shall mount up with
wings as eagles; they shall run, and not be
weary; and they shall walk and not faint.
—Isaiah 40:31 (KJV)

In Other Words...

As we depend on the Lord, He helps us. Sometimes
problems are simply lifted off our shoulders; other
times problems seem manageable, and we thrive;
then there are problems that almost overwhelm
us...yet, we are able to cope by God's grace.

FEBRUARY 5

All scripture is given by inspiration of God,
and is profitable for doctrine, for reproof,
for correction, for instruction in
righteousness.
—2 Timothy 3:16 (KJV)

In Other Words…

God communicated through His Holy Word
what He wants us to understand for our good; to
correct our thinking, and teach us what is right.

FEBRUARY 6

For you were once darkness, but now you are
light in the Lord. Walk as children of the light!
—Ephesians 5:8 (NKJV)

In Other Words…

Every one of us has practiced sneaking around with
the darkness of sin, until the Lord changed our desire
into walking in the sunlight of His Son's light!

FEBRUARY 7

For where your treasure is, there
your heart will be also.
—Luke 12:34 (NKJV)

In Other Words…

We need to choose carefully what we value most;
not possessions only, but actions that endure
and will bring honor and glory to God.

FEBRUARY 8

Be diligent to present yourself approved to God,
a worker who does not need to be ashamed,
rightfully dividing the word of truth.
—2 Timothy 2:15 (NKJV)

In Other Words...

Take care to please God, not the pressures of
peer groups, by following His Holy Word.

FEBRUARY 9

All we like sheep have gone astray; we
have turned, every one, to his own way;
and the Lord has laid on Him
the iniquity of us all.
—Isaiah 53:6 (NKJV)

In Other Words...

We have all "done our own thing" now and
again to our shame. Jesus took that shame
onto Himself, and gave Himself in our place
at His crucifixion on Calvary's cross, because
of His loving grace and mercy for us!

FEBRUARY 10

With men it is impossible, but not with God;
for with God all things are possible.
—Mark 10:27 (KJV)

In Other Words...

Alone we are bereft, but with God all is miraculously
manageable!

FEBRUARY 11

Therefore if any man is in Christ, he is a
new creature; old thing are passed away;
behold, all things are become new.
—2 Corinthians 5:17 (KJV)

In Other Words…

We become adopted children of God, when
we surrender our hearts to Jesus Christ our
Savior! We are born again by faith; old ways
are put away, and we become new,
inside and out!

FEBRUARY 12

Be strong and of good courage…for the
Lord your God, He is the One who goes
with you. He will not leave you nor
forsake you.
—Deuteronomy 31:6 (NKJV)

In Other Words…

You are not alone, if you are a friend of God!
No need to fear, He will always stay beside
you to give you strength and courage.

FEBRUARY 13

Trust in the Lord with all your heart; and lean
not on your own understanding; in all your ways
acknowledge Him, and He shall direct your paths.
—Proverbs 3:5-6 (NKJV)

In Other Words…

Faith is such an amazing gift from God; by
faith we are transformed! When the times of
testing come to each of us, God's children,
we can surrender to His directions. He leads
us to find peace beyond understanding.

FEBRUARY 14

For God hath not given us the spirit of fear; but
of power, and of love, and of a sound mind.
—2 Timothy 1:7 (KJV)

In Other Words...

As children of God, let us boldly accept His
gifts of power, and love, and a sound mind, to
thankfully live for His glory. Fear comes from
dismissing God's great goodness to us.

FEBRUARY 15

For God so loved the world, that He gave His only begotten Son, that whosoever believeth in Him should not perish but have everlasting life.
—John 3:16 (KJV)

In Other Words…

This is the sweetest love letter ever written! God loves every one of us so much that He came down from heaven in the human form of Jesus to be our Savior! By faith in His perfect life, His sacrificial death, and His glorious resurrection from the dead, we may all receive abundant life now and for eternity.

FEBRUARY 16

If you confess with your mouth the Lord Jesus
and believe in your heart that God has raised
Him from the dead; you will be saved.
—Romans 10:9 (NKJV)

In Other Words…

By faith in the truth of God's Holy Word we
can proclaim the wonder of Jesus' divine
life, death, and resurrection! Salvation is
not about what we have accomplished; it's
all about what Jesus has done for us!

FEBRUARY 17

Whatever things are true, whatever things are noble, whatever things are just, whatever things are pure, whatever things are lovely, whatever things are of good report, if there is any virtue, and if there is anything praiseworthy… meditate on these things.
—Philippians 4:8 (NKJV)

In Other Words…

We can change the channel of our thinking. There is no need to continually dwell on the bad news of happenings at home and abroad. There is so much more to consider! The genuinely encouraging events and actions, that occur daily, need to be treasured within our hearts and minds.

FEBRUARY 18

The Lord shall preserve thy going out and thy coming in from this time forth and even forevermore.
—Psalm 121:8 (KJV)

In Other Words…

Wherever we may be…inside or out, far away or near, young or old, God will be with us, His children, through all of life's journey; and on into eternity!

FEBRUARY 19

And the peace of God, which surpasses
all understanding will guard hearts
and minds through Christ Jesus.
—Philippians 4:7 (NKJV)

In Other Words...

In those moments just past panic when we don't
know what to do, may we remember to be still!
Jesus commanded even troubled water, "Be still!"
and there was calm. He is able to fill our hearts with
peace and serenity, when we rest within His will.

FEBRUARY 20

In the beginning God created the
heaven and the earth.
—Genesis 1:1 (KJV)

In Other Words…

Our minds become overwhelmed, when we attempt
to understand the creative splendor of God! How
He created the entire universe is beyond all human
comprehension. We are so small, and God is so
great! In 2 Peter 2: 22 we read, "Beloved, do not
forget this one thing, that with the Lord one day is
as a thousand years, and a thousand years as one
day." We stand in awe of the majesty of our Maker,
our merciful and loving Lord!

FEBRUARY 21

Your word I have hidden in mine heart,
that I might not sin against You.
—Psalm 119:11-12 (NKJV)

In Other Words…

May we memorize and treasure Your wonderful
promises! Your guidelines for abundant living
lead us to follow paths of righteousness and
salvation! O God, may we not sin against You by
failing to honor the truths of Your Holy Word.

FEBRUARY 22

Let the words of my mouth, and the meditations
of my heart, be acceptable in Your sight, O
Lord, my strength, and my Redeemer.
—Psalm 19:14 (NKJV)

In Other Words…

O Lord, may all that I say, or think about saying,
or doing, be pleasing to You. I'm depending
on your gracious strength and mercy!

FEBRUARY 23

I can do all things through Christ who strengths me.
—Philippians 4:13 (NKJV)

In Other Words…

Christ has given the perfect example to follow in any
circumstance that may come about in life. Alone, we
may feel genuinely lacking in courage. By faith, God's
children know His Holy Spirit within can change
things! Jesus promised, "I am with you always even
to the end of the age." He gives us the strength
to cope with whatever comes or doesn't come.

FEBRUARY 24

For I am not ashamed of the gospel of
Christ; for it is the power of God for
salvation to everyone who believes.
—Romans 1:16 (NKJV)

In Other Words…

There is no shame in having faith in God's love for
His children! He has communicated to us through the
inspired holy scriptures; by the majesty of the Trinity
of God, Jesus left heaven and came down to earth as
one of us to communicate completely His sacrificial
love and salvation for mankind; by His Holy Spirit
indwelling each believer, we can be comforted,
affirmed, and commune with God for all
eternity. The good news of God's love was
fulfilled through Jesus Christ our Savior!

FEBRUARY 25

If we confess our sins. He is faithful and
just to forgive us our sins, and to cleanse
us from all unrighteousness.
—1 John1:9 (KJV)

In Other Words…

How refreshing it is to have a cleansing bath!
Prayer is better than a bath! We need to humble
ourselves before our Maker, and ask for His merciful
forgiveness for the blunders and deliberate bad
actions we have done. Our Father is forever kind
to His children! He will remove all the guilt, and
refresh our spirits with His boundless love.

FEBRUARY 26

Jesus said to him, You shall love the Lord
thy God with all your heart, and with all
your soul, and with all your mind.
—Matthew 22:37 (NKJV)

In Other Words…

No holding back! Our love must be complete,
in response to God's grace in our lives! He
has never been stingy in His goodness to
each of His children. May we let our love for
Him spill over onto others for His glory!

FEBRUARY 27

Love suffers long and is kind; love does not envy;
love does not parade itself, is not puffed up.
—1 Corinthians 13:4 (NKJV)

In Other Words…

Tenderly, patiently, unselfishly is
true love demonstrated!

FEBRUARY 28

For this is the love of God, that we
keep His commandments.
—1 John 5:3 (KJV)

In Other Words…

This is a tall order…somehow we fail over
and again to be true to God's commandments.
Thankfully, His grace offers forgiveness for
our failures, if we but ask. Our hearts long
to show our love to God by our actions!

FEBRUARY 29

Therefore humble yourselves under the mighty hand
of God, that He may exalt you in due time, casting
all your care upon Him, for He cares for you.
—1 Peter 5:6-7 (NKJV)

In Other Words…

Let us bow our heads with humility before God,
and lay our burdens down before Him. Our loving
Lord is ready and able to lift us up again, in His
perfect time, with His strength and grace.

MARCH 1

Love your enemies, do good to them who
hate you, bless those who curse you, and
pray for those who spitefully use you.
—Luke 6:27-28 (NKJV)

In Other Words...

Our Lord Jesus forgave even those who
crucified Him! May we, by His example
and the Holy Spirit's nudging, treat
others with prayerful kindness and generosity.

MARCH 2

The Lord bless you, and keep you; the
Lord make His face shine upon you, and
be gracious to you; the Lord lift up His
countenance upon you, and give you peace.
—Numbers 6:24-26 (NKJV)

In Other Words...

O, the peaceful calm of feeling the warmth of
our Lord's nearness, assuring us of His love.

MARCH 3

Are not two sparrows sold for a copper coin?
And not one of them falls on the ground apart
from your Father's will. But the very hairs of your
head are all numbered. Do not fear therefore;
you are of more value than many sparrows.
—Matthew 10:29-31 (NKJV)

In Other Words...

Pluck a single hair from your head; God knows! He
knows about everything we may ever experience
or discover. He values all that He has created,
and His people are treasured beyond measure!

MARCH 4

Know that the Lord is God! It is He that
made us, and we are His; we are His
people, and the sheep of His pasture.
—Psalm 100:3 (KJV)

In Other Words…

We are not the "deciders", only the followers.
Like sheep, we belong to our Shepherd, who
lovingly cares for us and protects us.

MARCH 5

So teach us to number our days, that
we may gain a heart of wisdom.
—Psalm 90:12 (NKJV)

In Other Words...

Time seems to fly by, but only for a limited number
of days for each of us. Consider the worth of each
moment, and think carefully about its use.

MARCH 6

But as many as received Him, to them He
gave the right to become children of God,
to those who believe in His name.
—John 1:12 (NKJV)

In Other Words…

Faith is required to accept the reality of the
divinity of Jesus Christ, the only begotten
Son of God. The Holy Spirit assures us of our
need for forgiveness and salvation, in order
to become adopted children of God.

MARCH 7

Nor is there salvation in any other, for there
is no name under heaven given among
men by which we must be saved.
—Acts 4:12 (NKJV)

In Other Words...

Many good men have lived, but only one Savior!
Jesus left heaven to come down to earth, appearing
like one of us, to communicate the fullness of God's
love. He came to offer Himself for our salvation

MARCH 8

This is the day which the Lord hath made;
we will rejoice and be glad in it.
—Psalm 118:24 (KJV)

In Other Words…

Each new day is a gift from God. May our
thankfulness be expressed with a happy heart!

MARCH 9

For the wages of sin is death; but the gift of God
is eternal life through Jesus Christ our Lord.
—Romans 6:23 (KJV)

In Other Words...

God provided a way to help us from the
ultimate payment for our wrong doings! He
came down from heaven to offer the gift of
salvation through the sacrifice of His only
begotten Son, Jesus Christ, on Calvary's cross!

MARCH 10

And we know that all things work together
for good to them that love God, to them
who are the called according to His
purpose.
—Romans 8:28 (KJV)

In Other Words...

All things that happen may not seem
good to us. Still, for those who love God,
He causes good to come from them.

MARCH 11

Whatever your hand finds to do,
do it with your might.
—Ecclesiastes 9:10 (NKJV)

In Other Words...

May we do the best we can at all times,
as an honor to our Maker.

MARCH 12

Now faith is the substance of things hoped
for, the evidence of things not seen.
—Hebrews 11:1 (KJV)

In Other Words...

Faith is given to us by God with the gentle
nudging of the Holy Spirit, urging our hearts
to surrender to the truths of the Bible, and live
in awe of the infinite creations of our Maker.

MARCH 13

And you are complete in Him.
—Colossians 2:10 (NKJV)

In Other Words...

Alone we know that we are lacking, but
with God all things are possible.

MARCH 14

By this all will know that you are My
disciples, if you have love for one another.
—John 13:35 (NKJV)

In Other Words…

May the love of God fill our hearts until His love
spills over onto everyone, whether near or far away.

MARCH 15

Thy word is a lamp unto my feet,
and a light unto my path.
—Psalm 119:105 (KJV)

In Other Words…

Each step we take along life's journey is brightly
illuminated, by following God's blessed directions.

MARCH 16

For now we see through a glass, darkly;
but then face to face; now I know in
part; but then shall I know even
as also I am known.
—1 Corinthians 13:12 (KJV)

In Other Words…

Our comprehension now is hazy. A day will
come when we shall fully understand everything,
and we will be understood completely!

MARCH 17

You formed my inward parts; You covered
me in my mother's womb. I will praise
You, for I am wonderfully made.
—Psalm 139:13-14 (NKJV)

In Other Words...

How intricate and awesome are Your creative
powers, O God! Even before I was born, you
knew me and made good plans for my future.

MARCH 18

Fear thou not; for I am with thee; be not
dismayed; for I am thy God; I will strengthen
thee; yea, I will help thee; I will uphold thee
with the right hand of my righteousness.
—Isaiah 41:10 (KJV)

In Other Words…

Thank You for keeping Your children steady
through all that comes our way, Lord. We treasure
the promise of Your presence, giving comfort
and encouragement to sustain us always.

MARCH 19

For we are His workmanship, created in Christ
Jesus for good works, which God prepared
beforehand that we should walk in them.
—Ephesians 2:10 (NKJV)

In Other Words...

What affirmation for each of God's children! We
have been individually created for accomplishing
good works, which were planned for us by
Christ Jesus long before we began to dream.

MARCH 20

He restores my soul.
—Psalm 23:3 (NKJV)

In Other Words...

How blessed to be rehabilitated, put back together again, by our loving Creator! When devastating circumstances break our spirits, God comes to our rescue. His Holy Spirit tenderly heals us, with comforting enlightenment and gentle persuasion.

MARCH 21

For what will it profit a man if he gains the
whole world and loses his own soul?
—Mark 8:36 (NKJV)

In Other Words...

We focus repeatedly on acquiring
possessions, and our
insatiable desire for more. May we remember
to guard our highest priority of true value: the
treasure of a heart and mind full of faith.

MARCH 22

Behold, the tabernacle of God is with men,
and He will dwell with them, and they
shall be His people, and God himself shall
be with them, and be their God.
—Revelation 21:3 (KJV)

In Other Words...

What an awesome honor to realize that God desires
to come into our homes, into our hearts! Gladly
invite Him to come in and make Himself at home!
(!Mi casa es su casa!) My home is Your home! Put
out the WELCOME mat and humbly receive Him!
May we bless the Lord with thankful love and joy!

MARCH 23

The heavens declare the glory of God; and
the firmament shows His handiwork.
—Psalm 19:1 (NKJV)

In Other Words…

The splendor of the skies fills our hearts with
wonder. The varied glory of dawn, noonday,
sunset, or darkness repeatedly displays the
majesty of God's universal creative genius!

MARCH 24

The heart of the prudent acquires knowledge,
and the ear of the wise seeks knowledge.
—Proverbs 18:15 (NKJV)

In Other Words…

Tune our hearts with a desire to keep on learning
as long as we live, that we may broaden our
understanding. May we not listen to the clamor
of rubbish that clogs the mind, but concentrate
on blessed information that will enrich
our thinking.

MARCH 25

Two are better than one; because they have
a good reward for their labor. For if they
fall, one will lift up his companion.
—Ecclesiastes 4: 9-10 (NKJV)

In Other Words…

Friendship is a blessed gift from God. How
encouraging to be in the company of a trusted
friend to savor life's joys or sorrows together.
People need each other! What sweet comfort is
found in the strength and loving bond of an
understanding friend.

MARCH 26

Then behold, the veil of the temple was torn in two from the top to bottom; and the earth quaked, and the rocks were split.
—Matthew 27:51 (NKJV)

In Other Words...

In that incredible moment when our Lord Jesus breathed His final breath on Calvary's cross, the whole earth shuddered with sadness; the rocks cracked with grief. There is not a rock in creation that was not broken asunder by the impact of that sacrificial offering of God's Son Himself. Even the forbidding curtain of the temple was shredded apart, providing all mankind with permission to enter into a personal relationship with our Maker.

MARCH 27

For I know the thoughts that I think toward
you, says the Lord, thoughts of peace, and not
of evil, to give you a future and a hope.
—Jeremiah 29:11 (NKJV)

In Other Words...

What comfort to realize that God is thinking
about us with thoughts of peace and goodness!
His blessed plans for a hopeful tomorrow!

MARCH 28

God is a Spirit; and those who worship Him
must worship Him in spirit and truth.
—John 4:24 (NKJV)

In Other Words…

Beyond all the matter of life and the clutter
of our existence, comes within our hearts a
splendid awareness of unspeakable awe of God!
Silently we worship Him in true humility.

MARCH 29

Stand fast in the Lord, my dearly beloved.
—Philippians 4:1 (KJV)

In Other Words...

Hold on to faith in God! While the world
swirls and implodes around us, let us cling
to the loving promises of God's mercy.

MARCH 30

When wisdom enters your heart, and knowledge is
pleasant to your soul, discretion will preserve you;
Understanding will keep you.
—Proverbs 2: 10-12 (NKJV)

In Other Words…

Wisdom gives peace to the soul! Understanding
is a pleasant trait that comes with knowledge,
filling the heart with assurance and self-
control. Discretion adds to the gift of
wisdom.

MARCH 31

Open my eyes, that I may see wondrous things
from Your law.
—Psalm 119:18 (NKJV)

In Other Words…

We discover the value of obeying the inspired
Word of God, when we contemplate the
immeasurable reward of our faith.

APRIL 1

Indeed heaven and the highest heavens belong to the
Lord your God, also the earth with all that is in it.
—Deuteronomy 10:14 (NKJV)

In Other Words...

God is over all that is, or was, or will ever be!
He is our Creator, Redeemer, and Majesty
of all from the beginning into infinity.

APRIL 2

These things I have spoken unto you, that
in me ye might have peace. In the world
ye shall have tribulation; but be of good
cheer, I have overcome the world.
—John 16:33 (KJV)

In Other Words...

Quietly the Holy Spirit soothes our troubled
hearts, despite the chaos of the world, and
we rest within His transcendent peace.

APRIL 3

I know whom I have believed, and am
persuaded that He is able to keep that which I
have committed unto Him against that day.
—2 Timothy 1:12 (KJV)

In Other Words…

As children of God, we live with confidence
that His promises are true, for the Holy
Spirit blesses each heart with
assurance and peace.

APRIL 4

Beloved, do not forget this one thing, that
with the Lord one day is as a thousand
years, and a thousand years
as one day.
—2 Peter 3:8 (NKJV)

In Other Words...

Time seems confounding with some days
flying by, while others drag. In childhood the
conception of time moves at a slow pace, but
in adulthood time appears to rush along. God
measures time differently, for His is infinite.

APRIL 5

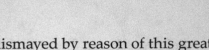

Be not afraid nor dismayed by reason of this great
multitude; for the battle is not yours, but God's.
—2 Chronicles 20:15 (KJV)

In Other Words…

When we realize the great force invading our
thinking through the impact of abounding
enticements is wrestling not only with us, but with
God Himself, we can take heart! Let us stay close
beside Him, for God will always be victorious.

APRIL 6

Let love be without hypocrisy. Abhor what
is evil. Cling to that which is good.
—Romans 12:9 (NKJV)

In Other Words…

May we hold on to all that is good and
true, and allow no place for falsehoods
of any kind, which lead only to
destruction.

APRIL 7

Faith cometh by hearing, and
hearing by the word of God.
—Romans 10:17 (KJV)

In Other Words...

With faith let us tell it again: God is love!
It is no secret! Let the whole world hear of
God's love for them! May we share the good
news of what Jesus has done for us.

APRIL 8

You are of God, little children,
and have overcome them,
because He who is in you is greater
than he who is in the world.
—1 John 4:4 (NKJV)

In Other Words...

We who by faith are the adopted children of God
can be stout hearted. By His grace we are filled
with a strength that only God can provide! He is
greater than any temptation the world offers.

APRIL 9

The Lord bless thee, and keep thee; the
Lord make His face shine upon thee, and
be gracious unto thee; the Lord lift up his
countenance upon thee, and give thee peace.
—Numbers 6:24-26 (KJV)

In Other Words…

Let us linger for a while in the splendor of God's
approval! As we bask in the realization that
blessings are being heaped upon us, may we
rejoice in the overflowing love of our heavenly
Father taking delight in His adopted child.

APRIL 10

The world is passing away, and the lust of it; but
he who does the will of God abides forever.
—1 John 2:17 (NKJV)

In Other Words...

The programmed obsolescence of things that many
scramble to attain pales in comparison with eternal
rewards promised to those who faithfully follow God!

APRIL 11

For we wrestle not against flesh and blood, but against principalities, against powers, against the rulers of the darkness of this world, against spiritual wickedness in the high places.
—Ephesians 6:12 (KJV)

In Other Words...

Life's journey can be dangerous; trouble confronts each of us around every corner. A duel is going on between good and evil, between darkness and light. May we always choose to be on God's side in order to be victorious!

APRIL 12

He who trusts his own heart is a fool; but
whoever walks wisely will be delivered.
—Proverbs 28:26 (NKJV)

In Other Words...

A fool chooses to please himself by playing
God's part. Those who are wise follow God's
leadership and are thankful always.

APRIL 13

Our soul waits for the Lord; He is our help and
our shield, for our heart shall rejoice in Him,
because we have trusted in His holy name.
—Psalm 33:20-21 (NKJV)

In Other Words…

May we take a deep breath when challenges
overtake us. May we find comfort, by
realizing that the Lord is our
protector! Trusting Him brings rejoicing.

APRIL 14

I will praise thee, O Lord, with my whole heart.
—Psalm 9:1 (KJV)

In Other Words...

From the moment of awakening, and
through each hour of the day, my heart will
be thankful for your goodness, O Lord!

APRIL 15

And we know that all things work together
for good to them that love God, to them
who are the called according to his
purpose.
—Romans 8:28 (KJV)

In Other Words…

God works things out for good, if we
love Him enough to give Him full
control and follow Him faithfully.

APRIL 16

For whatever is born of God overcomes
the world. And this is the victory that
overcomes the world...our faith.
—1 John 5:4 (NKJV)

In Other Words...

Faith in God leads to victorious living over all the
circumstances that come in life.

APRIL 17

Arise, shine; for your light is come! And the
glory of the Lord is risen upon you!
—Isaiah 60:1 (NKJV)

In Other Words…

Brighter than the shining of noonday will be
the splendor of heavenly light with the coming
of our Lord Jesus! His divine glory will arise
upon us, and even we shall shine with His
reflection.

APRIL 18

No temptation has overtaken you except such as is
common to man; but God is faithful, who will not
allow you to be tempted beyond what you are able;
but with the temptation will also
make a way of escape,
that you may be able to bear it.
—1 Corinthians 10:13 (NKJV)

In Other Words...

Overcoming temptation requires God's
help! On our own we are prone to failure.
Thankfully, God has promised to lead us
away from whatever the trouble may be,
if we will stay close beside Him.

APRIL 19

For the joy of the Lord is your strength.
—Nehemiah 8:10 (KJV)

In Other Words…

The more we consider what God has done for us, the more we are vitalized with abounding thanksgiving.

APRIL 20

Who shall separate us from the love of Christ?
—Romans 8:35 (KJV)

In Other Words...

No matter how high we may fly into
space, or how deep we may submerge
into the ocean, there is nothing that could
ever sever us from the love of Jesus.

APRIL 21

Approve things that are excellent; that ye may be
sincere and without offense till the day of Christ.
—Philippians 1:10 (KJV)

In Other Words…

Let us hold fast to all that is good
and true, as we follow
Jesus until the day He comes again.

APRIL 22

Fear thou not, for I am with thee; be
not dismayed, for I am thy God. I will
strengthen thee, yea, I will help thee.
—Isaiah 41:10 (KJV)

In Other Words...

How tenderly God reassures us of His protection
over us. Any time we become disheartened, He
promises to bless us with His loving care.

APRIL 23

For my thoughts are not your thoughts, neither are
your ways my ways, says the Lord, for as the heavens
are higher than the earth, so are my ways higher than
your ways, and my thoughts than your thoughts.
—Isaiah 55:8-9 (KJV)

In Other Words…

We cannot begin to comprehend the
majesty and creativity of our Maker! His
grandeur is beyond our human
imagination!

APRIL 24

Bless the Lord, O my soul; and all that is within
me bless His holy name! Bless the Lord, O
my soul, and forget not all His benefits.
—Psalm 103:1-2 (KJV)

In Other Words…

I will praise God with all my being; body, mind,
and soul. How can I begin to remember all His
blessings, countless as they have been in my life!

APRIL 25

For the law was given through Moses, but grace and truth came through Jesus Christ.
—John 1:17 (NKJV)

In Other Words…

We strive to not break the laws, for they were given by God to Moses for our good. Thankfully, Jesus provided us with grace and truth, blessing us with His unending love.

APRIL 26

Your eyes saw my substance, being yet
unformed; and in Your book they all were
written, the days fashioned for me.
—Psalm 139:16 (NKJV)

In Other Words...

Your foreknowledge of my entire life is
incomprehensible to my finite mind. You understand
me far better than I know myself! I am truly
thankful to have been included in Your book.

APRIL 27

It is of the Lord's mercies that we are not consumed,
because His compassions fail not. They are new every
morning; great is thy faithfulness.
—Lamentations 3:22-23 (KJV)

In Other Words...

God is faithful to heap new blessings upon His
children day by day. By His loving care we are
refreshed daily from the weariness of life.

APRIL 28

For You formed my inward parts; You
covered me in my mother's womb. I will
praise You, for I am fearfully and
wonderfully made; marvelous are Your works,
and that my soul knows very well.
—Psalm 139:13-14 (NKJV)

In Other Words...

We marvel at Your creative genius, which is
beyond human imagination. You fashioned us
within our mother's womb wondrously. In awe
we praise You for Your perfect provision!

APRIL 29

In the beginning was the Word, and the Word
was with God, and the Word was God.
—John 1:1 (KJV)

In Other Words…

God has been communicating with us from the
beginning of time! Through creation He revealed
Himself, through Jesus He revealed Himself, through
the Holy spirit He continues to reveal Himself.

APRIL 30

But seek ye first the kingdom of God,
and His righteousness; and all these
things shall be added unto you.
—Matthew 6:33 (KJV)

In Other Words...

For things to work smoothly, we must get them
together in proper working order: first things
first! So it is in our lives...we must seek God's
will for our lives, before we foolishly take off
on our own initiative. Our Father knows what
we need, and He will kindly guide us!

MAY 1

But it is good for me to draw near to God.
—Psalm 73:28 (KJV)

In Other Words...

It is our human nature to want to be near those we love. There is a longing beyond measure within us to draw near to God. His love is like a magnet pulling us toward Him. How good that a day is coming when we will be completely with Him in heaven!

MAY 2

Let all bitterness, and wrath, and anger,
and clamor, and evil speaking be put
away from you with all malice.
—Ephesians 4:31 (KJV)

In Other Words...

Jesus agonized on Calvary's cruel cross, suffering
anguish for the sins of all mankind; yet He found
the amazing grace to ask forgiveness for His
tormentors! His loving grace surpasses our human
understanding. Always He set perfect examples for
us, until His work on earth was finished. May we
show patience, kindness, and forgiveness to all, for
our challenges in life are only trifles by comparison.

MAY 3

Behold God is my salvation; I will
trust, and not be afraid.
Isaiah 12:2 (KJV)

In Other Words…

There is no place for timidity, or fear, for
God is our salvation! Shhhhh…be still
my heart; rest in blessed peace
now and forever.

MAY 4

He stores up sound wisdom for the upright; He is a shield to those who walk uprightly; He guards the paths of justice, and preserves the way of His saints.
—Proverbs 2:7-8 (NKJV)

In Other Words...

Whether we realize it or not, we are not alone! God has inspired His Holy Word to provide us with wisdom. When we follow His directions and seek the company of other people of faith, we find shelter and protection along the winding pathway of this life.

MAY 5

The heavens declare the glory of God; and
the firmament shows His handiwork.
—Psalm 19:1 (NKJV)

In Other Words...

Keep looking up! Throughout both daylight and
dark there is no end to the grandeur of God's
creation. We stand in awe of the infinity of the
universe as we gaze into the splendor of the skies.

MAY 6

For godliness with contentment is great gain.
—1 Timothy 6:6 (KJV)

In Other Words…

Great monetary wealth is desirable, but a greater
treasure is the contentment that comes with a
meaningful relationship with our Maker.

MAY 7

Ask, and it shall be given you; seek, and ye shall
find; knock, and it shall be opened unto you.
—Matthew 7:7-8 (KJV)

In Other Words...

God enjoys fellowship with His children.
When we pray to Him, we're sharing a close
personal relationship that is comforting. Our
Father knows what is most needful for us, and
the proper time for His gifts to be opened for
us. Within God's good company there's time
for expressing thanks and sharing our joys

MAY 8

We are His workmanship, created in Christ Jesus
for good works, which God prepared beforehand
that we should walk in them.
—Ephesians 2:10 (NKJV)

In Other Words...

Faith is paramount to believers, becoming the
essence of reality. We desire to glorify God
through every endeavor of our lives. May we
share the love of God through Jesus Christ,
knowing this is our purpose for existence.

MAY 9

Thou wilt show me the path of life; in
Your presence is fullness of joy; at Your
right hand are pleasures forevermore.
—Psalm 16:11 (NKJV)

In Other Words...

As we search the teachings of the Bible, we find that
God is communicating with us. He is revealing what
is good and pleasing in His sight, what works well,
and what does not. Those who humbly hear and
follow Him will find peace and joy are His reward.

MAY 10

You shall love the Lord your God with all your heart,
with all your soul, and with all your strength.
—Deuteronomy 6:5 (NKJV)

In Other Words...

We must never forget that our first priority is to
LOVE the Lord our God! Has He not heaped His
blessings upon us? Consider the wonder of our
five senses: the welcome gift of SIGHT revealing
to us the splendors of creation; the welcome gift
of SCENT, or the therapeutic gift of HEARING;
the pleasure of TASTE or the magic tingling of
TOUCH. Add to these marvelous gifts the fact
that God loves mankind so much He sent His only
begotten Son to demonstrate His great love for us!
When we think of Jesus' sacrifice at Calvary, who
could ever forget to love God with all your heart,
with all your soul, and with all your strength?

MAY 11

Be strong and of good courage; do not be
afraid, nor dismayed; for the Lord your
God is with you wherever you go.
—Joshua 1:9 (NKJV)

In Other Words…

We can do it! Whatever it is that may confront us
is possible to achieve, or to surmount, for we are
not alone. God has promised to be with us every
step along the winding way of life's journey.

MAY 12

Indeed heaven and the highest heaven belong to the
Lord your God, also the earth with all that is in it.
—Deuteronomy 10:14 (NKJV)

In Other Words...

Look up and consider this: everything that is
visible a far as the eye can see, and far beyond,
belongs to the Lord our God. His dominion is
greater than we are able to comprehend, or even
begin to fathom. O Lord, our Lord, how majestic is
Your name in all the earth...in all the universe!

MAY 13

Only fear the Lord, and serve him in
truth with all your heart; for consider how
great things He hath done for you.
—1 Samuel 12:24 (KJV)

In Other Words…

When we consider the grandeur of God, we
stand in awe! Deep within our thankful hearts
we long to please Him, knowing our life's chief
duty is to glorify God and enjoy Him forever.

MAY 14

The Lord does not see as man sees; for
man looks at the outward appearance,
but the Lord looks at the heart.
—1 Samuel 16:17 (NKJV)

In Other Words...

God has greater depth perception than we are able
to conjure. We are shallow in our comprehension
of others, easily impressed by decorations, but
God looks deeply into the hearts of one and all.

MAY 15

Give thanks unto the Lord, Call upon His name;
make known His deeds among the people.
—1 Chronicles 16:8 (KJV)

In Other Words...

Share the good news! Tell others what God has done
for you. Never cease to thank Him for His goodness
over all the earth,

MAY 16

If my people, which are called by My name,
shall humble themselves, and pray, and
seek My face, and turn from their wicked
ways; then I will hear from heaven, and will
forgive their sin, and will heal their land.
—2 Chronicles 7:14 (KJV)

In Other Words...

Turn! About face! Head in the right direction!
Obediently follow God's directions, not the devious
ways of the world. Be humble, and pray for a closer
walk with God. He promises to stay beside you,
and guide you to a place of healing and peace.

MAY 17

The Lord gave, and the Lord hath taken away;
blessed be the name of the Lord.
—Job 1:21 (KJV)

In Other Words...

Life on earth is given to us by God. It is only
temporary. Eternal life is the blessed promise
given by God to all who live by faith.

MAY 18

But You, O Lord, are a shield for me,
my glory and the One who lifts up my head.
—Psalm 3:3 (NKJV)

In Other Words…

You are my protector, and my hiding place,
O Lord. You uplift me by Your loving Holy
Spirit when I am feeling downcast.

MAY 19

When I consider Your heavens, the work
of Your fingers, the moon and the stars,
which You have ordained; what is man,
that that You are mindful of him.
—Psalm 8:3-4 (NKJV)

In Other Words...

The splendor of the skies is majestic far beyond
human comprehension. Scientists perceive that
our planet Earth is only the size of a grain of
sand within the magnitude of the galaxies of the
universe! Almost it seems incredible that You,
O Lord, would consider mankind even worth
considering.

MAY 20

Behold, I stand at the door, and knock. If any man hear My voice, and open the door, I will come in to him, and will sup with him, and he with me.
—Revelation 3:20 (KJV)

In Other Words…

What a great honor to have Jesus come over for dinner with us! He politely stops by, knocks, calls us by name, and awaits our invitation to be welcomed and received. May we embrace Him with love, encouraging Him to make His home with us forever!

MAY 21

But, beloved, do not forget this one
thing, that one day is with the Lord as a
thousand years, and a thousand years
as one day.
—2 Peter 3:8 (KJV)

In Other Words...

Our understanding does not equal God's
understanding. Time has no beginning and no end
with God. We live in the shadows of understanding,
whereas God is the fullness of light. Ponder His
greatness, and stand in awe of His majesty.

MAY 22

As each one has received a gift, minister
it to one another, as good stewards
of the manifold grace of God.
—1 Peter 4:10 (NKJV)

In Other Words...

Take joy in the gift God has given you! Celebrate
your gift by sharing it with others. To ignore
or hide the gift God has given you is to deny
having received it. Extend the blessing of your
gift from God by using it for the glory of God.

MAY 23

All flesh is as grass, and all the glory of man as the
flower of the grass. The grass withers, and the flower
falls away, but the word of the Lord endures for ever."
—1 Peter 1:24-25 (NKJV)

In Other Words...

We watch the seasons come and go. The flowers
bloom and fade away. Reluctantly, we see the changes
of our bodies as the years take their inevitable toll.
Only God's Holy Word remains consistently new.
It is applicable to every situation in life. Like Jesus
Christ, the same yesterday, today, and forever!

MAY 24

Every good gift and every perfect gift is
from above, and cometh down from the
Father of lights, with whom there is no
variableness, neither shadow of turning.
—James 1:17 (KJV)

In Other Words...

Today is another day for gift giving. Every day
is a day for gift giving from our loving Lord!
The bright lights of His generosity are always
turned "ON", never dimmed, or "OFF". How
good that God celebrates each day with perfect
gifts for His children.

MAY 25

For the word of God is quick, and powerful, and
sharper than any two-edged sword, piercing
even to the dividing asunder of soul and spirit,
and of the joints and marrow, and is a discerner
of the thoughts and intents of the heart.
—Hebrews 4:12 (KJV)

In Other Words...

God is in the changing business! By His Holy
Word our hearts and minds are pierced with
truth, probing deeply into the depths of our
souls. God knows what we need, and can
transform our iniquity into His righteousness!

MAY 26

Unto the pure all things are pure; but unto
them that are defiled and unbelieving is
nothing pure; but even their mind
and conscience is defiled.
—Titus 1:15 (KJV)

In Other Words...

The innocence of a child is a precious gift to
be treasured. Pornographic, vile presentations
rob the innocence of any child...never to be
recovered. Take care to guard what is allowed
within one's mind, or hearts and thoughts
become filled with pollution and corruption.
Choose carefully what is put into your mind!

MAY 27

Be diligent to present yourself approved
to God, a worker who does not need
to be ashamed, rightly dividing
the word of truth.
—2 Timothy 2:15 (NKJV)

In Other Words...

We are each responsible for what we dwell upon.
We can choose the subject matter that seems
most desirable. We have channel-changers to
facilitate the TV programming of our choice.
May we choose wisely, not foolishly, that each of
our selections will be pleasing in God's sight.

MAY 28

You will keep him in perfect peace,
whose mind is stayed on You.
—Isaiah 26:3 (NKJV)

In Other Words...

God is with you. Focus. Keep things in perspective.
The world may seem to be whirling out of
control; but that is not true. Be still, and know
that God is ultimately in full control! Consider
how perfectly the planets are poised in space,
and stand in awe of the grandeur of the universe.
The splendor of the heavens is only a reflection of
the majesty of God! Our hearts can each be filled
to overflowing with peace, as God is thankfully
praised for His wonderful love and provision.

MAY 29

He was wounded for our transgressions,
He was bruised for our iniquities; the
chastisement of our peace was upon Him,
and with His stripes we are healed.
—Isaiah 53:5 (KJV)

In Other Words…

Generations before Jesus was born of Mary
in Bethlehem, the prophet Isaiah foretold His
coming. Even the divine reason for His coming:
to become the ultimate sacrifice for our sins.
To think that Jesus would leave the glories of
heaven to provide this way for mankind to find
forgiveness from sin and salvation for eternity!
The love of God is beyond all measure!

MAY 30

You do not know what will happen tomorrow. For what is your life? It is even a vapor that appears for a little time and then vanishes away. Instead you ought to say, "If the Lord wills, we shall live and do this or that."
—James 4:14-15 (NKJV)

In Other Words…

We have no control over the events that surround us. We like to think we can schedule events and see them to fruition, but we can only respond to what God allows to happen. Our lives are a momentary poof in the passage of time, before we disappear. We would do well to remember that what our Lord wills is what is best! Humbly, let us seek His direction and follow His lead.

MAY 31

The effective, fervent prayer of a
righteous man avails much.
—James 5:16 (NKJV)

In Other Words...

Communication with God is how we stay in
touch with Him. We were created for divine
fellowship, companionship, and joy! The
blessing of courageous strength comes from
a close-knit relationship with our Maker.

JUNE 1

For our heart shall rejoice in him, because
we have trusted in His holy name.
—Psalm 33:21 (KJV)

In Other Words…

What joy fills our hearts, when we trust
completely! We know a peace and contentment
that is unparalleled. Only complete faith
in God can provide this holy blessing.

JUNE 2

There is therefore now no condemnation to them who
are in Christ Jesus, who walk not after the flesh,
but after the Spirit."
—Romans 8:1 (KJV)

In Other Words...

Breaking Good News for God's children! Our sin
debt has been paid in full by Jesus Christ our Savior!
We no longer have to carry that heavy burden of
guilt. We can walk within the Spirit of the One who
loved us so much He left heaven to die for us. Praise
God, Christ Jesus arose from the dead! By faith we
have been forgiven and saved for all eternity!

JUNE 3

I know whom I have believed, and am
persuaded that He is able to keep what I
have committed to Him until that day.
—2 Timothy 1:12 (NKJV)

In Other Words…

Confidence comes with trust. Trust comes with
faith. Faith comes with believing the word of an
honorable person. The gentleman most worthy
of our confidence is God Himself! The inspired
Word of God is treasured in the hearts of believers,
until that day we reach our final destination.

JUNE 4

Now may the God of peace Himself sanctify
you completely and may your whole spirit,
soul, and body be preserved blameless at
the coming of our Lord Jesus Christ.
—1 Thessalonians 5:23 (NKJV)

In Other Words...

What a blessed situation: to be cradled securely
within the arms of our heavenly Father, sheltered
by His love from the devious attractions of the
world. Only a child of God can experience this
holy peace for their body, mind, and soul.

JUNE 5

You are my hiding place and my
shield; I hope in Your word.
—Psalm 119:114 (NKJV)

In Other Words…

The safest place we can ever be is with God.
If we live according to His will, we can be
assured of His protection. His Holy Word
gives us that promise, and great hope.

JUNE 6

The Spirit of Him who raised Jesus from the dead dwells in you. He who raised Christ from the dead will also give life to your mortal bodies through His Spirit who dwells in you.
—Romans 8:11 (NKJV)

In Other Words...

O, the comfort of God's Holy Spirit within our hearts! Though our mortal bodies feel weak, He gives us strength. Though we are confounded by the complexities of existence, He gives us comfort. One day Jesus Christ will come to rescue each person of faith from this world's travail! Rest assured, we will be given the promised gift of eternal life with Him in glory, because of the indwelling of His Holy Spirit within our hearts.

JUNE 7

In Him was life and the life was the light of men.
—John 1:4 (KJV)

In Other Words...

Everything was brought into being by Him! All
that is, or was, or will one day become known to
man was made by the Creator of the universe;
holy, triune God the Father, Son, and Holy Spirit.
Life and light were blessedly given by Him
to perfectly sustain His marvelous work.

JUNE 8

In the beginning was the Word, and the Word
was with God, and the Word was God. The
same was in the beginning with God. All
things were made by Him, and without Him
was not any thing made that was made.
—John 1:1-3 (NKJV)

In Other Words…

O, the wonder of the Word of God! He communicates
with His people! Understanding the creation of
the heavens and the earth is awesome beyond our
human comprehension. Faith in the inspired Word
of God gives satisfaction to the hearts of believers.
While scientists progressively unravel findings of
worldly mysteries, the age old truths proclaimed
in the Bible are being positively confirmed. How
great is the Word of God! We stand amazed as
we witness the splendor of all nature and the
spheres resounding with majesty and praise!

JUNE 9

Prayers, intercessions, and giving thanks be made
for all men, for kings and all men in authority,
that we may lead a quiet and peaceable life
in all holiness and reverence, for this is good
and acceptable in the sight of God our Savior,
who desires all men to be saved and come
to the knowledge of the truth.
—2 Timothy 2:1-4 (NKJV)

In Other Words…

We need to pray for one another! We all need to
live a life that is acceptable in the sight of God
our Savior. Those in positions of national or local
leadership, persons who are part of the community,
as well as our individual families, are in urgent
need of an outpouring of God's Spirit of peace
and reverence for all mankind! May God save our
beloved country, as we acknowledge our need of
His truth, and give thanks with grateful hearts.

JUNE 10

For there is one God, and one Mediator between
God and men, the man Christ Jesus.
—1 Timothy 2:5 (KJV)

In Other Words...

Christ Jesus provided the bridge by which we
can reach God! He made our way possible by
His great sacrifice for our salvation on Calvary's
cross! Praise God from Whom all blessings flow!

JUNE 11

In all
these things we are more than conquerors through
Him that loved us.
—Romans 8:37 (KJV)

In Other Words…

The challenges of this life are not ours alone. Our
Lord and Savior loves us, and He has promised
to be with us through good times and bad. When
we feel faint or inclined to despair, He comes to
our rescue with strength and courage that only
He can give! Together, what a team we become!

JUNE 12

Rejoice in the Lord always; and again I will
say, rejoice! —Philippians 4:4 (KJV)

In Other Words...

Take heart! Let joy be consistent in your
thoughts, words, and deeds. Smile, in spite of
everything! Cheerfulness is contagious!

JUNE 13

These things I have spoken unto you, that
in Me ye may have peace. In the world
ye shall have tribulation; but be of good
cheer, I have overcome the world.
—John 16:33 (KJV)

In Other Words...

What a balm to our souls is this promise of Jesus!
The daily news reports are seldom about glad
happenings; there is trouble all over the world.
If we dwell only on the latest traumatic events,
depression could easily overtake us. Thankfully,
Jesus encourages us to be calm; the blessing of
peace is ours in the midst of the world's turmoil.

JUNE 14

You formed my inward parts; You covered me
in my mother's womb.
—Psalm 139:13 (NKJV)

In Other Words…

What some consider only a fetus is a miraculously
sheltered human life! By the genius of God's
creative design a new being is tenderly developing
that one day may accomplish good purposes
and great joys that could change the world.

JUNE 15

The grass withers, the flower fades, but
the word of our God stands forever.
—Isaiah 40:8 (NKJV)

In Other Words...

The inspired Word of God is always new,
applicable to every age! While other things grow
old, or come and go, the Word of God continues
to enlighten and give direction to mankind
through the ages past, present, and yet to come!

JUNE 16

Count it all joy when you fall into various
trials, knowing that the testing of your faith
produces patience. But let patience have its
perfect work, that you may be perfect
and complete, lacking nothing.
—James 1:2-4 (NKJV)

In Other Words…

Acquiring patience is a lifelong challenge
toward perfection. How earnestly we attempt,
but seldom succeed. Our Lord has told us to
"be still and know that I am God." Yet we rush
around and become harassed by the twists and
turns of life. May we pause and thankfully count
our blessings! Abundant life has been offered
to us that is lacking nothing, including joy and
patience through it all, made complete by faith.

JUNE 17

Then you shall call, and the Lord will answer;
you shall cry, and He will say, 'Here I am.'
—Isaiah 58:9 (NKJV)

In Other Words...

"O, Lord!" we cry when we are overwhelmed by
life. That call is not blasphemy, rather the urgent
need of a child for his loving Father. How reassuring
to recall God's promise, "Here I am." Strength
comes through the presence of the Holy Spirit
within each believer's heart, reminding us of His
blessed promise, "I will be with you always,
even to the end of the age."

JUNE 18

While we look not at the things which are seen, but at the things which are not seen; for the things which are seen are temporal; but the things which are not seen are eternal.
—2 Corinthians 4:18 (KJV)

In Other Words…

How easily we may be distracted. Events abound to claim our attention; disturbing "breaking news" seems incessant. Peer pressures and family desires could consume us with stress. As children of God, may we focus our attention on faithfulness, loving kindness, and joyful service to enrich the lives of others near and far, while thankfully using the talents we have been given to glorify God forever.

JUNE 19

Behold, God is my salvation, I will
trust and not be afraid; for the Lord
JEHOVAH is my strength and song.
—Isaiah 12:2 (KJV)

In Other Words...

I choose to place my faith in God, my Savior! Day by
day my heart is encouraged with new strength and
joy. Doubt may try to taunt me with discouragement,
but the blessed recall of God's loving promises fills
me with singing over the joy of my salvation!

JUNE 20

For a day in thy courts is better than a thousand. I would rather be a doorkeeper in the house of my God than to dwell in the tents of wickedness.
—Psalm 84:10 (KJV)

In Other Words…

What delight thrills our hearts when we enter the sanctuary of God's house filled with like-minded believers. Overwhelming holiness seems to permeate the room and each child of God. Hallelujah! To linger a while within the house of God never seems long; it is a treasure known to few around the world.

JUNE 21

For whoever exalts himself will be humbled,
and he who humbles himself will be exalted.
—Luke 14:11 (NKJV)

In Other Words…

Those who brag about their accomplishments
may soon be forgotten. Those who serve others
with kindness may be remembered with loving
gratitude through generations yet to come.

JUNE 22

And this is the love of God, that we keep His commandments. And His commandments are not burdensome. For whatever is born of God overcomes the world. And this is the victory that has overcome the world...our faith.
—1 John 5:3-4 (NKJV)

In Other Words...

We express our love for God by our obedience. The laws of God are for our good, to protect us and guide us in the ways that lead to victorious living. The gift of faith overcomes the world!

JUNE 23

For as the body without the spirit is dead,
so faith without works is dead also.
—James 2:26 (KJV)

In Other Words...

Faith and works belong together! Where there is no
spirit in the body, good works cannot exist. Good
works by the faithful are evidence of gratitude
to God for the blessings of His salvation.

JUNE 24

Do all things without complaining and disputing,
that you may become blameless and harmless,
children of God without fault in the midst of
a crooked and perverse generation, among
whom you shine as lights in the world.
—Philippians 2:14 (NKJV)

In Other Words…

As the children of God we are to worship Him, not
one another. Worship is the thankful expression
of joy for the blessing of God's salvation! Worship
styles may vary, leading to disputes, if we do
not focus our worship on serving God Himself.
Discord results when we gather together for our
personal satisfaction only. Let us light up the world
with the love of God, and worship will become
unbounded adoration to the glory of God.

JUNE 25

Truly my soul silently waits for God; from Him comes
my salvation; He only is my rock and my salvation;
He is my defense; I shall not be greatly moved.
—Psalm 62:1-2 (NKJV)

In Other Words…

Quietly I await God's loving protection. In
the shelter of His grace, I find peace amid
the whirling of this world's tumult. Praise
God from whom all blessings flow!

JUNE 26

I will sing of the mercies of the Lord
forever; with my mouth will I make known
Your faithfulness to all generations.
—Psalm 89:1 (KJV)

In Other Words…

With my mouth I will sing praises to You, O Lord.
With my mind I will consider Your mercies and
write praises to You, O Lord. With my soul I will
delight in Your marvelous creations, O Lord. I will
carry the torch of faith in You, O Lord, until that
day comes to hand it over to future generations.

JUNE 27

For Christ also suffered once for sins, the just for the unjust, that He might bring us to God, being put to death in the flesh but made alive by the Spirit.
—1 Peter 3:18 (NKJV)

In Other Words...

Jesus left the glories of heaven, coming down to earth in order to fulfill God's plan for the salvation of mankind. What sacrificial love! Perfect love, providing the way for unworthy sinners to receive His bridge of connection to God Himself! Jesus Christ accepted undeserved suffering and death, followed by His glorious resurrection, so we who trust in Him may be blessed with salvation and eternal life! No one but Jesus ever loved so!

JUNE 28

For to me to live is Christ, and to die is gain.
—Philippians 1:21 (KJV)

In Other Words...

Our purpose in life is to find joy in
glorifying God, and to discover the
splendors of God's heaven when we die.

JUNE 29

Put on the whole armor of God that ye may be able to stand against the wiles of the devil.
—Ephesians 6:11 (KJV)

In Other Words…

Be assured that needful protection comes with knowing the promises of God's Holy Word. The recall of Old and New Testament scriptures deflect the confusing trickery of worldly ways, which lead only to destruction.

JUNE 30

The fruit of the Spirit is love, joy, peace, longsuffering, kindness, goodness, faithfulness, gentleness, self-control. Against such there is no law.
—Galatians 5:22 (NKJV)

In Other Words…

O Lord, thank You for planting Your Holy Spirit deep within my heart! May Your Spirit thrive within me, I pray! Hope of a crop of Your beautiful fruit thrills my soul! It will take a miracle of Your grace for good fruit to come from my life. As Your love pours down like rain, I humbly anticipate growing into productivity for Your glory.

JULY 1

Let nothing be done through
selfish ambition or conceit,
but in lowliness of mind let each esteem others
better than himself.
—Philippians 2:3 (NKJV)

In Other Words…

We would be wise to kindly consider the opinions of
others, rather than try to force our biased opinions
upon others. The right may lie on the other side.

JULY 2

We are ambassadors for Christ, as
though God were pleading through us;
we implore you on Christ's behalf,
be reconciled to God.
—2 Corinthians 5:20 (NKJV)

In Other Words...

This is the urgent message we have been given
to share with the world: God loves you! He
showed His great love through Jesus Christ our
Savior, that all may find pardon for sin, and
receive His gift of abundant life eternally!

JULY 3

For now we see through a glass darkly, but then face to face; now I know in part; but then shall I know even as also I am known.
—1 Corinthians 13:12 (KJV)

In Other Words...

To know is to understand. Someday, when we reach our heavenly home, everything will become clear to us! The reason for whatever seemed incomprehensible will be understood, without question. Problems that seemed unsolvable before will be clarified, without a word spoken. We will all be understood! What comfort and joy that will bring to each of God's children; heavenly light in place of darkness!

JULY 4

No temptation has overtaken you except such as
is common to man; but God is faithful, who will
not allow you to be tempted beyond what you
are able, but with the temptation will make the
way of escape, that you may be able to bear it.
—1 Corinthians 10:13 (NKJV)

In Other Words...

Sometimes we are enticed to do things that we
know are not right for us. Gluttony, theft, substance
abuse, immorality, lying, selfish control to the
detriment of others, and more may be the options
we consider. Thankfully, our conscience, the Holy
Spirit in action, restrains us from the entrapment of
sinful behavior! Let God lead, and be shielded
from destruction.

JULY 5

For I am not ashamed of the gospel of
Christ, for it is the power of God unto
salvation for everyone that believeth.
—Romans 1:16 (KJV)

In Other Words...

Of what value is a secret Christian? With thankful
hearts, may those who are saved be bold to share
the good news of God's love for all mankind. Jesus
Christ came to prove that love once and for all...
by His sinless life, sacrificial death, and miraculous
resurrection from the dead! Praise God!

JULY 6

These things I have spoken unto you, that
in Me ye might have peace. In the world
ye shall have tribulation; but be of good
cheer, I have overcome the world.
—John 16:33 (KJV)

In Other Words...

We are inundated with each day's news. Not only
our family's complex doings, but local happenings,
and the events of our entire planet! There is so
much going on, the awareness of it can be very
stressful. We need to change the channel of our
thinking! Let's consider God's abundant love for His
children: peace and joy are His good gifts to us,
in spite of everything!

JULY 7

God is a Spirit, and they that worship Him
must worship Him in spirit and in truth.
—John 4:24 (KJV)

In Other Words…

Silently, how silently we become aware of God's
presence, through His Holy Spirit. The splendor of the
skies, both daytime and night presents His majesty,
as we stand in awe. The music of laughter and
sparkling contentment is revealed, as treasured loved
ones are held bone-close. His Holy Word restores
both strength and joy, through understanding at last.

JULY 8

In the beginning was the Word, and the Word
was with God, and the Word was God. The
same was in the beginning with God. All
things were made by Him, and without Him
was not any thing made that was made. In Him
was life, and the life was the light of men.
—John 1:1-4 (KJV)

In Other Words...

Word is communication! Our Triune God, the Father,
Son, and Holy Spirit is our great communicator! In
creation He spoke, and unfathomable wonders came
into being! He communicated His majesty for all to
see! In sending Jesus to earth for our salvation, He
communicated His merciful love for everyone! In the
Holy Spirit's coming, He communicates His love yet
again, constraining and empowering us for His glory!

JULY 9

One's life does not consist in the abundance
of the things he possesses.
—Luke 12:15 (KJV)

In Other Words…

The greatest treasures we have in life are not
purchases we have made. What really counts
and brings us joy is God's love and His countless
blessings of purpose, peace, and faith!

JULY 10

With men it is impossible, but not with God;
for with God all things are possible.
—Mark 10:27 (KJV)

In Other Words…

God is in the changing business. When we
feel downhearted and given to despair, may
we remember that He is able to overcome any
and everything in His perfect timing.
We need to be calm and pray on!

JULY 11

Come unto Me, all ye that labor and are heavy laden, and I will give you rest.
—Matthew 11:28 (KJV)

In Other Words…

Time for recess! We give ourselves a needful break, when we pause for a blessed time of prayer with our Lord Jesus. He will refresh us with His promised rest!

JULY 12

For I know the thoughts that I think toward you,
says the Lord, thoughts of peace and not of evil,
to give you a future and a hope.
—Jeremiah 29:11 (KJV)

In Other Words...

How kind of the Lord to think of each of us! To
think that He keeps the universe swirling in perfect
interplanetary order, even as He concentrates
thoughts of peace upon our future! How great is
our God to care for all His creation so tenderly!

JULY 13

Look at the birds of the air, for they neither
sow nor reap nor gather into barns; yet
your heavenly Father feeds them.
Are you not of more value than they?
—Matthew 6:26 (NKJV)

In Other Words…

God provides the air that surrounds us, giving us the
next breath we need to take. God provides the trees,
plants and animals, the teeming waters that provide
the nutrients we need for sustenance. Are we not
on a scavenger hunt upon the earth, finding God's
plentiful provisions, with much yet to be discovered?

JULY 14

We are the clay, and thou our potter;
and we are all the work of thy hand.
—Isaiah 64:8 (KJV)

In Other Words…

We are a work in process! Not one of us is yet
complete, polished, and ready for show and
tell. We're whirling on the potter's wheel, often
struggling against our Maker. Still, He holds us
firmly within His will, for our good and usefulness!

JULY 15

For lo, the winter is past, the rain is over and gone.
The flowers appear on the earth;
the time of the singing of birds is come.
—Song of Solomon 2:11-12 (KJV)

In Other Words...

With the coming of springtime, the earth seems
reborn with new life and beauty. What was barren
becomes abundant with foliage and flowering
fruitfulness! By God's grace, even we feel a new
lease on life, with renewed purpose for living!

JULY 16

How much better is it to get wisdom
than gold! And to get
understanding is to be chosen rather than silver.
—Proverbs 16:16 (NKJV)

In Other Words...

Wisdom and understanding take years to acquire!
A measure of patience, careful observation,
and thoughtful meditation precede these truly
treasured qualities. May we aspire to possess
the sympathetic spirit of peace that leads
to wisdom.

JULY 17

You, O Lord, are a shield for me,
my glory and the One
who lifts up my head.
—Psalm 3:3 (NKJV)

In Other Words…

As we take our place within the front lines of living,
Lord, we thank You for Your protection from the
worldly ways that would damage, even destroy, us!
You lead us by Your grace, and fill us with guidance
and encouragement when we might despair.

JULY 18

We are His workmanship, created in Christ Jesus for good works, which God prepared beforehand that we should walk in them.
—Ephesians 2:10 (NKJV)

In Other Words...

It is good to be needed. Having a purpose in life gives great satisfaction. Knowing God has planned good works for us to accomplish is an awesome consideration! We may become useful tools pre-planned to bless lives for His eternal glory.

JULY 19

For the word of God is quick, and powerful, and
sharper than any two-edged sword, piercing
even to the dividing asunder soul and spirit,
and of the joints and marrow, and is a discerner
of the thoughts and intents of the heart.
—Hebrews 4:12 (KJV)

In Other Words…

How powerful is the communication between
God and man! When His Holy Word reaches
deep into our hearts, the wonder of our response
is beyond full comprehension. Soon, or later, the
realization comes that we have been impacted,
directed, guided into the fullness
of abundant living by
understanding!

JULY 20

And we know that all things work together for good
to them that love God, to them who are the called
according to His purpose.
—Romans 8:28 (KJV)

In Other Words...

Those who love God strive to do what is
pleasing in His sight. When our hearts are
rightly aligned with His will and purpose, we
may be assured that God will bless our
situation, confounding as it may be. Through it all,
good will triumph!

JULY 21

There is therefore now no condemnation
to those who are in Christ Jesus, who do
not walk according to the flesh,
but according to the Spirit.
—Romans 8:1 (NKJV)

In Other Words...

Free at last! Praise God, we can be free at last!
No more must we live under condemnation for
the muddle we've made of our sin-prone lives!
Through the loving sacrifice of Jesus Christ our
Savior, our sins are forgiven by faith! We are saved
by grace; His Spirit reassures us day after day
as we live on!

JULY 22

Let the word of Christ dwell in you richly, in all wisdom, teaching and admonishing one another in psalms and hymns and spiritual songs, singing with grace in your hearts to the Lord.
—Colossians 3:16 (KJV)

In Other Words…

Tell it again! Over and over again! God loves you! Claim His loving promises for your very own! Let your heart sing with encouragement and thankfulness for His blessings! Praise God from Whom all blessings flow! Let joy ring from your life!

JULY 23

Whatever you want men to do to you, do also to them.
—Matthew 7:12 (NKJV)

In Other Words...

We are to be kind to one another. There is nothing good that comes from returning evil for evil! Let's stretch ourselves and discover that God will help us replace anger with peace, greed with generosity, hatred with love. Such actions are a challenge worth taking, for we are not alone; God is with us.

JULY 24

He who walks with integrity walks securely.
—Proverbs 10:9 (NKJV)

In Other Words...

We can almost skip along with the confidence of a gymnast taking the next step on a narrow beam, assured of what to do next! Skill can only come from practicing what is known to be right!

JULY 25

He shall cover thee with His feathers,
and under His wings you shall take refuge.
—Psalm 91:4 (NKJV)

In Other Words...

How tenderly our heavenly Father cares for His
children! His Holy Spirit inspired the writings that
shelter us with the protection of great wisdom. We
may thankfully turn to them for security, amid
the challenging circumstances of our lives!

JULY 26

Thanks be to God, which gives us the victory,
through our Lord Jesus Christ.
—1 Corinthians 15:57 (NKJV)

In Other Words...

Whatever success we may enjoy comes from
what Jesus has done for us! He is our benefactor;
we are those benefited by His marvelous grace
and goodness. What a victory over sin and death
came through our Lord and Savior, Jesus Christ;
presently, in times past, and in future days to come!

JULY 27

There is nothing that enters man from outside, which can defile him; but the things which come out of him, those are the things that defile a man.
—Mark 7:15 (NKJV)

In Other Words…

Words need to be weighed very carefully, for they can be our making, or breaking. Words have the potential to wound, or heal, in powerful ways! It's not what we eat or drink that damages our character. But what we say without thinking about those who are listening that is most destructive.

JULY 28

Set your affection on things above,
not on things on the earth.
—Colossians 3:2 (KJV)

In Other Words...

May we focus our awareness on all that is beautiful
and good! Let us resist dwelling on the multitude
of earthly problems, for negative thinking pulls
us down, entrapping our minds like quicksand.

JULY 29

Two are better than one...for if they fall,
one will lift up his companion.
—Ecclesiastes 4:9-10 (NKJV)

In Other Words...

We need one another! God did not plan for
His children to be solitary beings. We are
blessed to delight in one another by loving
and helping them, just as we are blessed
by others also.

JULY 30

And He is before all things and
by Him all things consist.
—Colossians 1:17 (KJV)

In Other Words…

Triune God the Father, God the Son, God the
Holy Spirit was before anything else existed.
Our human minds cannot comprehend such
majesty! Everything that exists was
created by God. God the Father
designed His universal
creation; God the Son carried out His divine plan;
God the Holy Spirit affirms His reality.

JULY 31

Oh, give thanks unto the Lord; call upon his name;
make known His deeds among the people.
—Psalm 105:1 (KJV)

In Other Words…

How can we begin to thank God for His majesty
and grace? Continually, in times past, presently,
and in days to come He showers mankind with
His blessings! Let us delight in Him always, with
thanksgiving for His deeds throughout the ages.

AUGUST 1

Love does no harm to a neighbor;
therefore love is the fulfillment of the law.
—Romans 13:10 (NKJV)

In Other Words…

God's Holy Word teaches us to love, and never
do harm. Love is needed everywhere, always!

AUGUST 2

He only is my rock and my salvation.
—Psalm 62:2 (KJV)

In Other Words…

We scurry about seeking pleasure and
acceptance. Look to Jesus, and discover
joy and eternal love to build
your life upon!

AUGUST 3

We are ambassadors for Christ, as though God were
pleading through us; we implore
you on Christ's behalf be
reconciled to God.
—2 Corinthians 5:20 (NKJV)

In Other Words…

Hear me, I pray. For your sake, and God's
glory, find peace for all time and eternity
through faith in Jesus Christ
our Savior!

AUGUST 4

"For my thoughts are not your thoughts,
neither are your ways my ways," saith
the Lord. "For as the heavens are
higher than the earth, so are My ways higher than
your ways, and My thoughts than your thoughts."
—Isaiah 55:8-9 (KJV)

In Other Words

We cannot see into the future, or know our coming
response in any given situation. Not so with our
heavenly Father; all things are known by Him!
Foreknowledge is part of His incredible majesty!
What a mercy it is to live only in the present moment;
foreknowledge would overwhelm us! God is so
great! High beyond our human ability to fully
comprehend!

AUGUST 5

The earth is the Lord's, and the fullness thereof;
the world and they that dwell therein.
—Psalm 24:1 (KJV)

In Other Words...

Our planet Earth and everything within it belongs
to God. Our marvelous universe with all its'
splendor belongs to Him. As do we, one and all!

AUGUST 6

Now the Lord God of hope fill you with
all joy and peace in believing, that ye may
abound in hope through the power
of the Holy Ghost.
—Romans 15:13 (KJV)

In Other Words…

By the power of God's Holy Spirit, believers
may be filled with hope, joy, and peace!

AUGUST 7

You should earnestly contend for the faith, which was once delivered unto the saints.
—Jude 1:3 (KJV)

In Other Words…

Those who accept the gift of faith, which was delivered to all, hold it treasured!

AUGUST 8

Put on the tender mercies, kindness,
humility, meekness,
long-suffering.
—Colossians 3:12 (NKJV)

In Other Words...

Tender mercies are never rude or vain; but kind,
humble, meek, and patient with one and all.

AUGUST 9

Have you not known? Have you not heard?
The everlasting God, the Lord, the Creator
of the ends of the earth, neither faints nor is
weary? His understanding is unsearchable.
—Isaiah 40:28 (NKJV)

In Other Words…

Do you not know that God, the everlasting
creator of all that was, or is, or ever will
be, does not tire or grow weary? His
majesty is beyond all comprehension!

AUGUST 10

Command those who are rich in this present age not to be haughty, nor to trust in uncertain riches but in the living God, who gives us richly all things to enjoy.
—1 Timothy 6:17 (NKJV)

In Other Words...

Never forget that every blessing comes from God our Father. His goodness is heaped upon us, for God is constant in His caring.

AUGUST 11

Forgetting those things which are behind, and
reaching forth unto those things which are
before, I press toward the mark for the prize
of the high calling of God in Christ Jesus.
—Philippians 3:13-14 (KJV)

In Other Words…

No matter the past, we can look forward to
completing what God has planed for us to accomplish
in this life; for His glory and our eternal good.

AUGUST 12

The grass withers, the flower fades, but
the word of our God stands forever.
—Isaiah 40:8 (NKJV)

In Other Words…

The flowers of springtime fade
with the coming of Fall,
but God's Holy Word is forever fresh!

AUGUST 13

The Lord is my light and my salvation;
whom shall I fear? The Lord is the strength
of my life; of whom shall I be afraid?
—Psalm 27:1 (KJV)

In Other Words...

There is no darkness when we stay
within the light of the Lord, where we are
protected and have no need to fear.

AUGUST 14

I am the vine you are the branches. He
that abides in Me, and I in Him, the same
bears much fruit; for without Me
you can do nothing.
—John 15:5 (NKJV)

In Other Words…

When we are grafted into the branches of
everlasting life, through faith in Jesus Christ
our Savior, we begin to bear good fruit for His
glory. Without Him we could do nothing.

AUGUST 15

Blessed be God, which hath not
turned away my prayer,
nor His mercy from me.
—Psalm 66:20 (KJV)

In Other Words…

God is so good to hear our prayers
and sustain us with His mercy!

AUGUST 16

For what profit is it to a man if he
gains the whole world,
and loses his own soul?
—Matthew 16:26 (NKJV)

In Other Words…

First things first; let us place honoring God
as our highest priority! Any substitute
would only lead to loss for our soul.

AUGUST 17

These things I have spoken unto you, that in Me ye
have peace. In the world ye shall have tribulation;
but be of good cheer; I have overcome the world.
—John 16:33 (KJV)

In Other Words...

Trouble surrounds us, yet our Lord Jesus transcends
the travail of this world by His countless joys.

AUGUST 18

The righteous, are bold as a lion.
—Proverbs 28:1 (KJV)

In Other Words…

By faith, God's children become lion-hearted!

AUGUST 19

And the Word was made flesh, and dwelt
among us, and we beheld his glory, the
glory as of the only begotten of the
Father, full of grace and truth.
—John 1:14 (KJV)

In Other Words…

Abundant wonders of Godly communication
came to us through Jesus Christ, the only
begotten Son of God. When He came to live as
one of us, Jesus showed His perfection, with
forgiveness and salvation for all mankind. The
truth of triune divinity became known after
Jesus' sacrificial death on Calvary's cross; for our
beloved Jesus Christ, Messiah, was miraculously
resurrected from the dead! Alleluia! Amen.

AUGUST 20

And the Word was made flesh, and dwelt among us, and we beheld his glory, the glory as of the only begotten of the Father, full of grace and truth.
—John 1:14 (KJV)

In Other Words...

The trinity of God was revealed through the coming of Jesus Christ for the forgiveness of mankind. By faith in His virgin birth, perfect life of grace and truth, sacrificial death, and miraculous resurrection from the dead, we begin to comprehend the love of God for His children. The Holy Spirit persuades our hearts of the need for salvation through faith and obedience.

AUGUST 21

This Book of the Law shall not depart from your
mouth, but you shall meditate in it day and night, that
you may observe to do according to all that is written
in it. For then you will make your way prosperous,
and then you will have good success. Be strong and
of good courage; do not be afraid, nor be dismayed,
for the Lord your God is with you wherever you go..
—Joshua 1:8-9 (NKJV)

In Other Words…

There is a hunger in each of us to thrive. We
attempt to satisfy this desire in various ways,
sometimes to our distress. The recipe for the food
we truly need is the Bread of life: the inspired
Word of God. It was lovingly provided to help
us find the way to achieve successful living!

AUGUST 22

Thy testimonies are wonderful; therefore doth my soul keep them. The entrance of thy words giveth light; it giveth understanding unto the simple.
—Psalm 119:129-130 (KJV)

In Other Words...

It is necessary for us to consider things carefully. Understanding, through enlightenment, is a wonderful treasure to be sought! All things become clearer through the light of God's Holy Word.

AUGUST 23

He who heeds the word wisely will find good.
And whoever trusts in the Lord, happy is he.
—Proverbs 16:20 (NKJV)

In Other Words...

Let us attempt to see others as the Lord sees them.
We will be able to love others more, even as He does.
Through His wisdom the Lord perceives good that is
not apparent. Happy are those who trust in the Lord!

AUGUST 24

The secret things belong unto the Lord our God, but those things, which are revealed belong unto us and to our children for ever, that we may do all the words of this law.
—Deuteronomy 29:29 (KJV)

In Other Words...

O Lord, how kind that You chose to reveal all that is needful for us to know! Hold us in the calm of Your goodness and mercy as we trust in You, awaiting the revelation of secret things You have chosen to keep.

AUGUST 25

The Lord shall preserve thy going out and thy coming
in from this time forth, and even for evermore.
—Psalm 121:8 (KJV)

In Other Words…

We are under God's protection, wherever we may be.
He stays with us even when we wander
about and stumble into danger. God rescues
us time and again, as we learn to allow
Him to be the kindly guide of our life.

AUGUST 26

Fear not; for I am with thee; be not dismayed; for
I am your God. I will strengthen you. Yes. I will
uphold you with My righteous right hand.
—Isaiah 41:10 (NKJV)

In Other Words...

What a comfort to reach out to our Father God
when life is overwhelming. To feel the strength
of His protection, when we are in need, is
reminiscent of our childhood feeling of security
in the nearness of a caring parent. Beyond
that human blessing is the love of God!

AUGUST 27

Most assuredly, I say to you, He who hears
My word and believes in Him who sent Me
has everlasting life, and shall not come into
judgment; but has passed from death into life.
—John 5:24 (NKJV)

In Other Words...

Everybody needs to know! Far and near, young
and old need to hear, believe, and live with faith
in Jesus' words! The truth He mercifully promises
includes the forgiveness of sins, plus an awesome
waver from judgment, purchased by His sacrificial
death and resurrection, that we may be able to go
from death into everlasting life with Him in glory!

AUGUST 28

As every man hath received the gift, even so
minister the same one to another, as good
stewards of the manifold grace of God.
—1 Peter 4:10 (KJV)

In Other Words...

Each and every one of us has received a gift, a unique
talent, from God. We may be slow to discover what
our gift might be, but one happy day it will become
apparent! We need to be thankfully bold, and realize
that divine gifts given carry a responsibility. God
does not provide a secret for us to have and timidly
hide, but a ministry for us to share with others.
The talent may be minuscule, but good stewards
find it changed by the manifold grace of God!

AUGUST 29

Thou shalt have no other gods before Me.
—Exodus 20:3 (KJV)

In Other Words…

We tend to crave things; hopefully, not to the point
of worship! O, Lord, we ask forgiveness for our
tendency to desire this, that, or the other. Have
we become insatiable? The "specials" promoted
repeatedly take our fancy! We may begin to
consider such temptations to be priorities, even
necessities. With the words of an old hymn, let us
pause and pray as we sing, "the things of earth
will grow strangely dim in the light of His glory
and grace." We worship only You, dear God!

AUGUST 30

The secret things belong unto the Lord our
God, but those things, which are revealed
belong unto us and to our children forever,
that we may do all the words of the law.
—Deuteronomy 29:29 (KJV)

In Other Words…

We cherish the Word of God that we are
able to comprehend, for our faith is greatly
enriched. We want to hand down Godly truths
to our children for guidance in their lives.
Yet, there is much in the Word of God that
remains a mystery to us. Lord, help us accept
the secret things that belong to You only.

AUGUST 31

Do not be afraid, nor be dismayed, for the Lord
your God is with you wherever you go.
—Joshua 1:9 (NKJV)

In Other Words…

How comforting to be reassured that we are not
alone on this journey of life! What a blessing to
trust the Lord is beside us, protecting us from
the pitfalls that confront those who choose to
live their own way. God will take care of you!

SEPTEMBER 1

Let those also who love Your name be joyful in
You, for You, O Lord, will bless the righteous; with
favor You will surround him as with a shield.
—Psalm 5:11-12 (NKJV)

In Other Words...

How pleasant it is to feel the closeness of
the Lord! To be at ease within His love
and protection fills the heart with
comforting peace and joy!

SEPTEMBER 2

The Lord does not see as a man sees; for
man looks at the outward appearance,
but the Lord looks at the heart.
—1 Samuel 16:7 (NKJV)

In Other Words...

How quickly we are impressed by snap
judgments! God sees fully, deep down inside
us! We can be fooled by outward appearances,
but God knows what lies within the heart
of each of us. May beauty lie within!

SEPTEMBER 3

Indeed heaven and the highest heavens belong to the
Lord, your God, also the earth with all that is in it.
—Deuteronomy 10:14 (NKJV)

In Other Words…

We came into this world with nothing. God
provided everything we would ever need.
Our Lord looked upon all that He had created
throughout the universe, and He said "It is good!"
May we trust Him and know that we are blessed
with enough; for God has lovingly provided.

SEPTEMBER 4

Yet who knows whether you have come to
this kingdom for such time as this?
—Esther 4:14 (NKJV)

In Other Words...

Consider what is confronting us. At this
very moment in time, our actions may
change the course of life's journey.
Ponder carefully the value of the influence
we may have on those near and dear to
us. Breathe deeply; take courage!

SEPTEMBER 5

In Him we have redemption through
His blood, the forgiveness of sins,
according to the riches of His grace.
Ephesians 1:7 (NKJV)

In Other Words...

Jesus left heaven's glory to come to earth, that we
might be redeemed. He humbled Himself to become
the unblemished offering sacrificed for the salvation
of all mankind. The richness of His grace cannot be
measured! The blood that Jesus shed covers the sins
of faithful believers! We are mercifully forgiven and
changed forever into acceptable children of God.

SEPTEMBER 6

For to me, to live is Christ, and to die is gain.
—Philippians 1:21 (KJV)

In Other Words…

What a blessed transformation! The Christ-filled
life is enriched even more within eternity.

SEPTEMBER 7

Wisdom is the principal thing; therefore get wisdom,
and with all thy getting get understanding.
—Proverbs 4:7 (KJV)

In Other Words...

We seek education and knowledge, because we want
to be smart, don't we? The principal thing we need is
understanding, which will lead us to obtain wisdom.

SEPTEMBER 8

To every thing there is a season, and a
time to every purpose under heaven.
Ecclesiastes 3:1 (KJV)

In Other Words...

In springtime the wonder of new life occurs
all around us miraculously. With summer
comes the joy of abundance with fruition and
harvesting. Fall sheds the earth's splendor of
plenty, leaving enough for sufficient provision.
Winter brings a time for quiet rest and welcome
restoration of spent energies. Changing seasons
reveal the purposes of heaven for all creation!

SEPTEMBER 9

Yet I will rejoice in the Lord,
I will joy in the God of my salvation.
—Habakkuk 3:18 (NKJV)

In Other Words…

In the midst of everything, the joy of the Lord
brings strength and peace to my heart!

SEPTEMBER 10

He hath made everything beautiful in its time.
—Ecclesiastes 3:11 (NKJV)

In Other Words…

Patience is necessary for growth. A bud brings forth a
beautiful flower, slowly, but surely.

SEPTEMBER 11

For whoever exalts himself shall be humbled,
and he that humbles himself will be exalted.
—Luke 14:11 (NKJV)

In Other Words…

It is vain to pretend that we are high and mighty. One
must be steady and faithful to ultimately be esteemed.

SEPTEMBER 12

"Try Me now in this," says the Lord of hosts. "If I will not open to you the windows of heaven and pour out for you such blessings that there will not be room enough to receive it."
—Malachi 3:10 (NKJV)

In Other Words…

Trust in the Lord's overflowing goodness of abundant provisions, as we hold fast to our faith in Him and His merciful blessings.

SEPTEMBER 13

And the Holy Spirit descended in bodily
form like a dove upon Him, and a voice
came from heaven which said, "You are My
beloved son; in You I am well pleased."
—Luke 3:22 (NKJV)

In Other Words…

What a moment in time, when God miraculously
revealed His pleasure in His divine Son! Glory came
down as the voice of God was heard in affirmation of
Jesus, proclaiming heaven's blessing of loving favor!

SEPTEMBER 14

Verily, verily, I say unto you, he that heareth
my Word, and believeth on Him that sent Me,
hath everlasting life, and shall not come into
condemnation; but is passed from death unto life.
—John 5:24 (KJV)

In Other Words…

Listen carefully, and fully trust in the inspired word
of God! Believe in the marvelous trinity of God, as
revealed through Jesus Christ, that His love may
redeem your soul from death and gain eternal life!

SEPTEMBER 15

Let us therefore come boldly unto the
throne of grace that we may obtain mercy
and find grace to help in time of need.
—Hebrews 4:16 (KJV)

In Other Words…

We have an open invitation to feel welcome
in expressing our needs to our Father in
heaven. He is lovingly generous with His
abundant mercy and grace, and desires a
personal relationship with His children.

SEPTEMBER 16

Do not let your adornment be merely outward…
arranging the hair, wearing gold, or putting
on fine apparel…rather let it be the hidden
person of the heart, with the incorruptible
beauty of a gentle and quiet spirit, which
is very precious in the sight of God.
—1 Peter 3:3-4 (NKJV)

In Other Words…

Try as we may to present ourselves with
fashionable outward finery, true beauty always
comes from within the heart! Precious in the sight
of God and man is a gentle and quiet spirit!

SEPTEMBER 17

Fear not, for I am with you; be not dismayed, for I am your God. I will strengthen you, yes. I will help you. I will uphold you with My righteous right hand.
—Isaiah 41:10 (NKJV)

In Other Words...

Be still my soul. Stay calm, knowing that assuredly God is with us, just as He promised. How blessed to live in faith, strengthened by His presence!

SEPTEMBER 18

Come unto me, all ye that labor and are
heavy laden, and I will give you rest.
—Matthew 11:28 (KJV)

In Other Words…

Time for recess! We all need "time out" from
the challenges of the day! Welcome rest and
relaxation await us when we yield our body, mind,
and soul to the Holy Spirit's healing control.

SEPTEMBER 19

Come now, you who say, "Today or tomorrow we will go to such and such a city, spend a year there, buy and sell, and make a profit"; whereas you do not know what will happen tomorrow. For what is your life? It is even a vapor that appears for a little time and then vanishes away. Instead you ought to say, "If the Lord wills, we shall live and do this or that."
—James 4:13-15 (NKJV)

In Other Words...

We are not the decider, or decision maker, of what is to come. Our lives are but a vapor that comes and goes for a time; what do we fully comprehend? Thankfully, we are within God's merciful control! Humbly, may we acknowledge Him with "God-willing" before our actions.

SEPTEMBER 20

Since we are surrounded by so great a cloud
of witnesses, let us lay aside every weight, and
sin which so easily ensnares us, and let us run
with endurance the race that is set before us.
—Hebrews 12:1 (NKJV)

In Other Words...

Let's keep on keeping on! May we be encouraged
to run the race of life with our best efforts,
blessed by the reality of countless saints of all
the ages cheering us on to victory in Jesus!

SEPTEMBER 21

Aspire to lead a quiet life, to mind your own
business, and to work with your own hands.
—1 Thessalonians 4:11 (NKJV)

In Other Words…

The clamor of traumatic events surrounds each of
us. We may counter such happenings by taking
the time to be creative with any talent God has
bestowed upon us. We may sew, or sing, garden,
or play a musical instrument, cook or write…
the options are endless; and truly beneficial!

SEPTEMBER 22

I can do all things through Christ who strengths me.
—Philippians 4:13 (NKJV)

In Other Words…

Let us never despair! When we feel lacking,
breathe deeply and remember Who has promised
to be with us through whatever comes in life.
The strength of the Holy Spirit of our Lord
Jesus is made perfect in our weakness.

SEPTEMBER 23

But the fruit of the Spirit is love, joy, peace, long-suffering, gentleness, goodness, faith, meekness, temperance; against such there is no law.
—Galatians 5:22-23 (KJV)

In Other Words…

Acceptable by acclimation are the blessed attributes of the gifts of the Holy Spirit, as revealed in the lives of the faithful! Gladly the world would welcome such admirable traits in one and all!

SEPTEMBER 24

For ye know the grace of our Lord Jesus Christ, that
though He was rich, yet for your sakes he became
poor, that ye through his poverty might be rich.
—2 Corinthians 8:9 (KJV)

In Other Words…

Amazing grace! Our Lord Jesus Christ left the
riches of heaven, clothing Himself in lowly
humanity for our salvation. By faith in His loving
sacrifice on Calvary's cross and His glorious
resurrection from the dead, we become rich!
His everlasting love is beyond measure.

SEPTEMBER 25

For now we see through a glass, darkly; but then face to face; now I know in part; but then shall I know even as also I am known.
—1 Corinthians 13:12 (KJV)

In Other Words...

To see and know, to fully understand, and be understood! What a wonderful difference from the murky view we have of people and things on earth in the here and now! With the completion of our time on earth, all things will become new and blessed by God with beauty and compassion.

SEPTEMBER 26

Now abide faith, hope, love, these three;
but the greatest of these is love.
—1 Corinthians 13:13 (NKJV)

In Other Words…

Whatever our ages, wherever we abide,
whatever our aspirations may be, to love and
be loved is life's greatest aim and treasure!

SEPTEMBER 27

How beautiful are the feet of them that
preach the gospel of peace, and bring
glad tidings of good things!
—Romans 10:15 (KJV)

In Other Words…

How beautiful to see those coming who share
the blessing of peace! Once together, we hear of
the best things life has to offer. We sing and pray
and join together in fervent praise of God who
loved us all, through Jesus Christ, our Savior.

SEPTEMBER 28

Nevertheless He left not Himself without witness, in that He did good, and gave us rain from heaven, and fruitful seasons, filling our hearts with food and gladness.
—-Acts 14:17 (KJV)

In Other Words...

Every man, woman, and child is witness to the wonder of God's love! His goodness is evident all around us, with rain for refreshment from heaven, seasons of fruitfulness to sustain us, and blessings that fill our lives with joy and gladness.

SEPTEMBER 29

But God forbid that I should glory, save in the
cross of our Lord Jesus Christ, by whom the world
is crucified unto me, and I unto the world.
—Galatians 6:14 (KJV)

In Other Words...

How can we ever say enough about the love
of our Lord Jesus Christ? He left the glories
of heaven to come down to earth and live
among us, ultimately offering himself for our
salvation by faith in His divinity! Words cannot
suffice. We must live to love Him forever.

SEPTEMBER 30

Until now you have asked nothing in my name. Ask, and you will receive, that your joy may be full.
—John 16:24 (NKJV)

In Other Words…

By praying in the name of Jesus, we would only ask for what He knows is best. What we may think we'd enjoy, and even ask for, may not be what Jesus knows would be best. The key to receiving is asking in Jesus name for what He knows is best; abundant joy will follow!

OCTOBER 1

If you then being evil, know how to give good gifts
to your children, how much more will your heavenly
Father give the Holy Spirit to those who ask Him?
—Luke 11:13 (NKJV)

In Other Words...

What delight we take in surprising our children
with gifts to thrill their hearts! We may enjoy their
pleasure even more than they do. How much more is
God pleased to give us the gift of His Holy Spirit to
comfort and guide us with blessed goodness always!

OCTOBER 2

Verily, I say unto you, Inasmuch as ye have done it unto one of the least of these my brethren, ye have done it unto me.
—Matthew 25:40 (KJV)

In Other Words…

It's the little things that really matter. Our Lord does not expect us to perform grand accomplishments to fulfill His expectations. Jesus treasured the little children, and He clearly assures us of His appreciation for small deeds of kindness we extend to those in need; each is a pleasing gift in His honor!

OCTOBER 3

Call unto Me, and I will answer thee, and show you
great and mighty things, which you do not know.
—Jeremiah 33:2 (NKJV)

In Other Words…

Keep in touch! What a kind invitation from
our maker to communicate personally! As we
share our questions and longings with Him,
we become aware of His will and His mighty
wonders all around, far beyond our imaginings!

OCTOBER 4

Seek the Lord while he may be found, and
call ye upon him while he is near.
—Isaiah 55:6 (KJV)

In Other Words…

Seize the moment while the presence of God is near!
This opportunity may not come again. God is present
and waiting for you now; patiently, waiting for you.

OCTOBER 5

Know therefore that the Lord thy God, he is God, the faithful God, which keeps covenant and mercy with them that love him and keep his commandments to a thousand generations.
—Deuteronomy 7:9 (KJV)

In Other Words…

God is faithful to keep His promises down through the generations of those who love and obey Him. With mercy He keeps His covenant with those who live by faith.

OCTOBER 6

"For My thoughts are not your thoughts,
neither are your ways My ways," says the
Lord, "For as the heavens are higher than the
earth, so are My ways higher than your ways,
and My thoughts than your thoughts."
—Isaiah 55:8-9 (KJV)

In Other Words…

Beyond all our imaginings are the ways of our
Lord. We cannot begin to fathom the heights or
the depths of God's plans for our good and for
His glory. Our thoughts are infinitesimally small,
but His thoughts are immeasurably great!

OCTOBER 7

Charm is deceitful and beauty is passing, but a woman who fears the Lord, she shall be praised.
—Proverbs 31:30 (NKJV)

In Other Words…

We may be fooled by the charm of beauty for a time, but a woman whose heart is filled with awe of the Lord is not fooling around. She is worthy to be praised.

OCTOBER 8

Bless the Lord O my soul; and all that is within
me, bless his holy name, Bless the Lord, O
my soul and forget not all His benefits.
—Psalm 103:1-2 (KJV)

In Other Words…

With all my heart I praise You, O Lord! With all
my being I praise You and bless Your holy name.
Your merciful benefits are immeasurable; they are
too many to begin to recall! My soul is beyond
blessed by Your loving goodness, O Lord!

OCTOBER 9

If My people which are called by My name, shall humble themselves, and pray, and seek My face, and turn from their wicked ways; then will I hear from heaven, and will forgive their sin, and heal their land.
—2 Chronicles 7:14 (KJV)

In Other Words...

May we children of God gather together and humbly pray for God's intervention in the midst of our troubles. May our wicked ways be turned away from, and repented, that we may find God's merciful forgiveness! May our land be healed, we humbly pray.

OCTOBER 10

It is of the Lord's mercies, that we are not consumed,
because his compassions fail not. They are new
every morning; great is thy faithfulness.
—Lamentations 3:22-23 (KJV)

In Other Words…

God so kindly restores us each time we feel
overwhelmed by circumstances! His compassion
never fails; great is our Lord's faithfulness! Each
morning we are refreshed by His new mercies!

OCTOBER 11

Lay not up for yourselves treasures upon earth, where moth and dust doth corrupt, and where thieves break through, and steal; but lay up for yourselves treasures in heaven, where thieves do not break through nor steal; for where your treasure is, there will your heart be also.
—Matthew 6:19-20 (KJV)

In Other Words...

Our most valuable treasures lie within our hearts. Nothing can take away love, joy, kindness, mercy, or compassion! These treasures may be stored safely for the day of our welcome homecoming to heaven!

OCTOBER 12

For the law was given through Moses, but grace and truth came through Jesus Christ.
John 1:17 (NKJV)

In Other Words...

The laws of the 10 Commandments are most excellent guidance and clear directions for living a righteous life. Still, we fail over and again to abide within them. How good of God to bless us with His grace and truth through Jesus Christ to save us from our sinful worldly ways!

OCTOBER 13

Search me, O God, and know my heart; try me and know my thoughts; and see if there be any wicked way in me, and lead me in the way everlasting.
—Psalm 139:23-24 (KJV)

In Other Words...

As You look into my heart, O God, You see my countless imperfections! I pray You will forgive me, and keep me near You. Lead me in Your way of everlasting goodness that I may be as You intended.

OCTOBER 14

We are the clay, and You our potter; and
all we are the work of Your hand.
—Isaiah 64:8 (NKJV)

In Other Words...

Hold me close, dear Lord. I whirl around the wheel
of life and would fly off, if Your strong hand does not
restrain me. Make me become something useful in
Your hands, I pray; something pleasing in Your sight.

OCTOBER 15

When you do a charitable deed, do not let your left hand know what your right hand is doing that your charitable deed may be in secret; and your Father who sees in secret will Himself reward you openly.
—Matthew 6:3-4 (NKJV)

In Other Words...

Secrets are just between You and me, Lord, no one else needs to know! What is done is not for show, to impress others or gain attention; what is done is for Your eyes only, that something good may come to be.

OCTOBER 16

Return to your own house and tell what
great things God has done for you.
—Luke 8:39 (NKJV)

In Other Words…

Good news is worth repeating. Those
nearest and dearest need to hear about the
joy of God's goodness in our lives!
A thankful heart gladly gives glory to God.

OCTOBER 17

As many as received Him, to them He
gave the right to become children of God,
to those who believe in His name.
—John 1:12 (NKJV)

In Other Words…

To be adopted into the family of God by faith
makes us the children of God! The merciful
gift of salvation, through Jesus Christ,
provides assurance of heaven's heritage.

OCTOBER 18

As the Father hath loved me, so have I
loved you; continue in my love.
—John 15:9 (KJV)

In Other Words…

We are loved, even as God loved His Son!
May we never stray away from the comforting
peace of His divine love. Welcome one
and all, whether near or far away, into the
blessed shelter of God's everlasting love.

OCTOBER 19

There is none righteous, no, not one.
—Romans 3:10 (KJV)

In Other Words…

We have all been a disappointment. We aren't consistently obedient, not a single one of us! We try to get by on our own, or do what we know to be wrong. Thankfully, God is so good; faithful to forgive, when we turn away from our foolishness.

OCTOBER 20

Blessed be God the Father of our
Lord Jesus Christ, the
Father of mercies, and the God of all comfort;
who comforts us in all our tribulations, so
that we may be able to comfort those who are
in any trouble, with the comfort with which
we ourselves are comforted of God.
—2 Corinthians 1:3 (NKJV)

In Other Words...

Praise God, when we have experienced the blessed
comfort of God's mercies in our times of trouble, we
are enabled to help others in their times of need.

OCTOBER 21

In Him we have redemption through
His blood, the forgiveness of sins,
according to the riches of His grace.
—Ephesians 1:7 (NKJV)

In Other Words…

Revealing His amazing love for all mankind,
Jesus Christ left the glories of heaven to become
the ultimate blood sacrifice for the forgiveness
of sin. By faith in His living divinity, we
are redeemed by His incredible grace!

OCTOBER 22

To the only wise God, our Savior, be
glory and majesty, dominion, and power,
both now and forever. Amen.
—Jude 1:25 (KJV)

In Other Words...

Before and beyond all else, God our Savior is in
control with divine wisdom, glory, majesty, dominion,
and power over everything, everywhere, forever!

OCTOBER 23

But ye are a chosen generation, a royal priesthood,
an holy nation, a peculiar people; that ye should
show forth the praises of him who hath called
you out of darkness into His marvelous light.
—1 Peter 2:9 (KJV)

In Other Words...

Truly honored are we children of God, chosen
to represent our Father, by sharing the good
news of His love for all, and reflecting His
marvelous light in the midst of darkness.

OCTOBER 24

Gird up the loins of your mind, be sober, and
rest your hope fully upon the grace that is to be
brought to you at the revelation of Jesus Christ.
—1 Peter 1:13 (NKJV)

In Other Words…

It is necessary to take control of our tossing minds,
resting fully in faith, by the grace
of our Lord Jesus Christ.

OCTOBER 25

We do not lose heart. Even though our outward man is perishing, yet the inward man is being renewed day by day.
—2 Corinthians 4:16 (NKJV)

In Other Words...

We will keep on keeping on! Weary as we may be, God renews our spirit day by day.

OCTOBER 26

For we know that if our earthly house, this tent, is destroyed, we have a building from God, a house not made with hands, eternal in the heavens.
—2 Corinthians 5:1 (NKJV)

In Other Words…

When our earthly dwelling place is beyond repair, God has prepared a splendid new home for us in heaven. On homecoming day we shall be blessed with a divine welcome, as we move into our heavenly home for all eternity.

OCTOBER 27

Oh, the depth of the riches both of the wisdom
and knowledge of God! How unsearchable are
His judgments and His ways past finding out!
—Romans 11:33 (KJV)

In Other Words...

The things of God are beyond imagining by
our finite minds! The riches of His wisdom and
knowledge are unsearchable by one and all.

OCTOBER 28

For where two or three are gathered together in
My name, there am I in the midst of them.
—Matthew 18:20 (KJV)

In Other Words…

When we gather together to praise God,
His love overflows from within our hearts.
The blessed presence of His Spirit abounds
and joy is wondrously increased.

OCTOBER 29

He who is not with Me is against Me, and he
who does not gather with Me scatters.
—Luke 11:23 (NKJV)

In Other Words...

Whose team shall we choose? The sidelines
are not a position to be taken. By caring for
others, we gather them together to find faith
in God. By ignoring others, we scatter them
away to never find faith in God. Our actions
will prove if we are for, or against God.

OCTOBER 30

Let us therefore come boldly unto the
throne of grace that we may obtain mercy,
and find grace to help in time of need.
—Hebrews 3:16 (KJV)

In Other Words…

"Fear not," are gracious words Jesus spoke, to all
believers. We may boldly respond to His words
of loving encouragement, knowing He will share
His mercy and grace just when we need it most.

OCTOBER 31

Go ye therefore and teach all nations, baptizing them
in the name of the Father, and of the Son, and of
the Holy Ghost; teaching them to observe all things
whatsoever I have commanded you, and, lo, I am
with you always, even unto the end of the world.
—Matthew 28:19-20 (KJV)

In Other Words...

Jesus gave His great commission to
believers, that faith in Him could be shared
with all mankind; promising He would
be with us throughout life's journey.

NOVEMBER 1

Herein is love, not that we loved God,
but that He loved us, and sent his Son
to be the propitiation for our sins.
—1 John 4:10 (KJV)

In Other Words…

We love God, because He first loved us! It is
by Him that all things beautiful came into
being…all things wonderful were created…
all things good were demonstrated by His
grace. God's love was perfectly revealed by the
self-giving of our Redeemer, Jesus Christ!

NOVEMBER 2

When I consider Your heavens, the work of Your fingers, the moon and the stars, which You have ordained, what is man that You are mindful of him?
—Psalm 8:3-4 (NKJV)

In Other Words...

I stand amazed by Your majesty, O Lord! The splendor of the universe is far beyond my comprehension! You are so great and I am so small! Your loving provision for creation is an incredible blessing of Your grandeur!

NOVEMBER 3

He who heeds the Word wisely will find good,
and whoever trusts in the Lord, happy is he.
—Proverbs 16:20 (NKJV)

In Other Words…

When we trust in the truth of God's Holy Word, our
indecisiveness becomes settled. We find peace in our
hearts, true happiness, because our faith is complete.

NOVEMBER 4

We are all as an unclean thing, and all our
righteousnesses are as filthy rags.
—Isaiah 64:6 (KJV)

In Other Words…

Our best efforts are dingy from the stains
of egocentric motives within most life
endeavors. How we need the cleansing
strength of God's mercy and goodness to
purify our intentions and ultimate actions.

NOVEMBER 5

Call to me, and I will answer you, and show you
great and mighty things, which you do not know.
—Jeremiah 33:3 (NKJV)

In Other Words...

How thankful I am that You invited me to call to
You anytime! Only You know what lies ahead;
the wonderful plans You have for my future.
Your answers come with gentle guidance and
courage to journey on through the mighty
discoveries of life.

NOVEMBER 6

For whom he did foreknow, he also did predestinate
to be conformed to the image of His Son, that he
might be the firstborn among many brethren.
—Romans 8:29 (KJV)

In Other Words...

You, O God, foreknew all that You created!
That is beyond our human comprehension.
"God-willing" affirms that mankind is to
conform to the perfection that Jesus so faithfully
demonstrated. When that miracle is accomplished,
our predestination will be heaven on earth!

NOVEMBER 7

Now the Lord is the Spirit; and where the
Spirit of the Lord is, there is liberty.
—2 Corinthians 3:17 (KJV)

In Other Words...

May we break away from the malaise of our idle
consciousness to the freedom of allowing the
Spirit of God to rouse within us an awareness
of His divine plan for our energies. The Holy
Spirit liberates us from the mundane into a
holy contemplation of what is truly significant
for life's highest purposes to be attained.

NOVEMBER 8

Let nothing be done through selfish ambition
or conceit, but in lowliness of mind let each
esteem others better than himself.
—Philippians 2:3 (NKJV)

In Other Words...

May we never crowd others out by
promoting our own selfish agenda. May
we be mindful of the value of all God's
children; affirming them to succeed,
using their God-given
talents.

NOVEMBER 9

And this is His commandment, that we should
believe on the name of His Son Jesus Christ, and
love one another, as He gave us commandment.
—1 John 3:23 (KJV)

In Other Words…

We are given God's divine directives for our
good, and His glory, leading us to the wondrous
results of peace and joy! The love of God was
fully revealed in His Son Jesus Christ, who gave
Himself for our salvation. By faith, we are to
love one another, just as God first loved us.

NOVEMBER 10

Behold what manner of love the Father has bestowed
on us, that we should be called children of God.
—1 John 3:1 (NKJV)

In Other Words...

We were not born the children of God; we are
the adopted children of God. How honored to
have been chosen of God, by faith, to become
a part of His family! We will be included
with the saints of all the ages, and His only
begotten Son Jesus, our blessed Redeemer!

NOVEMBER 11

The Lord bless thee and keep thee; the
Lord make his face shine upon thee, and
be gracious unto thee; the Lord lift up his
countenance upon thee, and give thee peace.
—Numbers 6:24-26 (KJV)

In Other Words…

The blessing of the Lord's Spirit overshadows my
being as these words are spoken. The light of His love
shining down permeates even the surroundings. The
holiness of His presence soothes the very depth of my
body, mind, and soul with His gracious gift of peace.

NOVEMBER 12

The joy of the Lord is your strength.
—Nehemiah 8:10 (KJV)

In Other Words…

May we count it all joy to awaken each morning,
eager to welcome the new day, refreshed
by the Lord's strength; thankful to serve in
whatever way His Holy Spirit may lead!

NOVEMBER 13

The heavens declare the glory of God; and
the firmament shows His handiwork.
—Psalm 19:1 (NKJV)

In Other Words...

The splendor of the heavens at dawn or setting sun
is magnificent to behold! Such majestic formations
imbued with colors that continually change, even
as they rearrange within the sky. Only God could
create such marvelous patterns of exquisite design!

NOVEMBER 14

He that covers his sins will not prosper; but whoever
confesses and forsakes them will have mercy.
—Proverbs 28:13 (NKJV)

In Other Words...

How foolish to think we could hide our sins
from Your view, Lord; all-knowing, almighty
God! Have mercy I humbly pray, and forgive
me for my waywardness. May my actions
and intentions be pleasing in Your sight, and
hiding from You never a consideration.

NOVEMBER 15

Here is what I have seen: it is good and fitting for one to eat and drink, and to enjoy the good of all his labor in which he toils under the sun all the days of his life which God gives him; for it is his heritage.
—Ecclesiastes 5:18 (NKJV)

In Other Words…

Our heavenly Father takes delight in what He has planned for us: to live, prosper, and take pleasure in the accomplishment of worthy endeavors. To relish the rewards of purposeful living is our blessed heritage!

NOVEMBER 16

Grow in the grace and in the
knowledge of our Lord and
Saviour Jesus Christ. To Him be glory
both now and for ever. Amen.
—2 Peter 3:18 (KJV)

In Other Words...

There is more! More grace to receive, more
knowledge to comprehend! Our Lord and Savior
Jesus Christ, has an unending abundance of
goodness to bestow upon believers! To Him be
all praise and glory forevermore! Amen!

NOVEMBER 17

This is the victory that has overcome
the world…our faith.
—1 John 5:4 (NKJV)

In Other Words…

To receive the gift of faith is life's greatest
treasure! Faith is offered to everyone, but
there are those who fail to accept it; who never
receive the gift of faith to find that grace,
mercy, love, and strength are also included.
Victorious living comes with the gift of faith!

NOVEMBER 18

For the word of God is living, and powerful, and
sharper than any two-edged sword, piercing
even to the division of the soul and spirit,
and of joints and marrow, and is a discerner
of the thoughts and intents of the heart.
—Hebrews 4:12 (NKJV)

In Other Words…

We ponder the word of God and sometimes
struggle to understand what is being revealed.
We feel challenged by truths that unsettle our
hearts and minds, causing immeasurable pain and
discomfort. We know the things of God are the
things of God; His Holy Spirit will unravel our
confusion at the proper time. Let us be still, and
know that God will help us, just as He promised.

NOVEMBER 19

So then faith cometh by hearing and
hearing by the word of God.
—Romans 10:17 (KJV)

In Other Words...

There is work to be done! Everybody needs to
know that God loves every one of us! We need to
go and tell! The inspired writings of the Holy Bible
record God's love through His miraculous works
through the ages. The Bible is His Story! When
God's love is known, faith will change the world!

NOVEMBER 20

But God forbid that I should glory, save in the
cross of our Lord Jesus Christ, by whom the world
is crucified unto me, and I unto the world.
—Galatians 6:14 (KJV)

In Other Words...

How can we ever say enough about the love
of our Lord Jesus Christ? He left the glories
of heaven to come down to earth and live
among us, ultimately offering himself for our
salvation by faith in His divinity! Words cannot
suffice. We must live to love Him forever.

NOVEMBER 21

I will both lie down in peace and sleep; for You alone, O Lord, make me dwell in safety.
—Psalm 4:8 (NKJV)

In Other Words...

To sleep undisturbed...what a blessing! The serenity of such bliss happens when our being is surrounded by safety. Only with You, O Lord, do we find this peace.

NOVEMBER 22

In the beginning, God created
the heaven and the earth.
—Genesis 1:1 (KJV)

In Other Words...

Our minds become overwhelmed, when we
attempt to understand the creative splendor of
God. How He created the entire universe is beyond
all human comprehension! We are so small, and
God is so great! In 2nd Peter 3: 8 we read: "Beloved,
do not forget this one thing, that with the Lord
one day is as a thousand years and a thousand
years as one day." We stand in awe of the majesty
of our Maker, our merciful and loving Lord!

NOVEMBER 23

We all, with open face, beholding as in a glass the
glory of the Lord, are changed into the same image
from glory to glory, even as by the Spirit of the Lord.
—2 Corinthians 3:18 (KJV)

In Other Words...

A glance into the mirror now
reveals an image I hardly
recognize. There appear to be aging changes,
yes, but no transformation into glory is visible
upon my unveiled face! I am still a work in
progress; the Spirit of the Lord may make His
blessed changes in a time yet to come.

NOVEMBER 24

For this is the love of God, that we keep His commandments. And His commandments are not burdensome. For whatsoever is born of God overcomes the world. And this is the victory that has overcome the world…our faith.
—1 John 5:3-4 (NKJV)

In Other Words…

We express our love for God by our obedience. The laws of God are given for our good, to protect us and guide us in the ways that lead to victorious living. The gift of faith overcomes the world!

NOVEMBER 25

The Lord is near to those who have a broken heart; and saves such as have a contrite spirit.
—Psalm 34:18 (NKJV)

In Other Words…

How tenderly You restore my spirit, O Lord, when times of sadness surround me. The discouragements that would break my heart are replaced by the promises of Your Holy Word! My soul is encouraged by Your grace.

NOVEMBER 26

Likewise the Spirit also helps in our weaknesses.
For we do not know what we should pray for as we
ought, but the Spirit Himself makes intercession.
—Romans 8:26-27 (NKJV)

In Other Words…

At times we may feel unable to express our
feelings, becoming mute from heavy burdens
that seem unutterable. Though our broken spirit
is silent, the Holy Spirit earnestly intercedes
with prayers on our behalf. We take heart,
knowing we will never be abandoned, for within
us abides the comfort of the Holy Spirit!

NOVEMBER 27

For God so loved the world, that He gave His only
begotten Son that whosoever believeth in Him should
not perish, but have everlasting life. For God sent
not His Son into the world to condemn the world,
but that the world through Him might be saved.
—John 3:16-17 (KJV)

In Other Words…

How could Jesus leave the glories of heaven
to become a child of humanity in order to
become the ultimate sin offering that would,
by faith, reconcile believing mankind to God?
How can such love ever be measured?

NOVEMBER 28

The Lord is my light and my salvation;
whom shall I fear? The Lord is the strength
of my life; of whom shall I be afraid?
—Psalm 27:1 (KJV)

In Other Words…

The LIGHT of the Lord dispels the darkness of
worldly opinions! The popular acceptance of
permissive behaviors, promoting whatever feels good
to be the truth, ultimately leads to destruction. Only
the inspired Word of God reveals what is Right or
Wrong! For salvation and strength for courageous
living, the Bible sheds blessed light upon the
direction to the Way, the Truth, and the Life.

NOVEMBER 29

Now may the God of hope fill you with all joy
and peace in believing, that you may abound
in hope by the power of the Holy Spirit.
—Romans 15:13 (NKJV)

In Other Words…

Hope is more than positive thinking! Hope is
trusting in the inspired Word of God! What joy
and peace this gives to the heart of believers!
We have abundant confidence by the power of
the Holy Spirit; hope for all our tomorrows!

NOVEMBER 30

All flesh is as grass, and all the glory of man as the flower of the grass. The grass withers and its flower falls away, but the word of the Lord endures forever.
—1 Peter 1:24 (NKJV)

In Other Words...

We are temporary residents on this earth. The length of our lives may be counted in days or decades. They are precious few in the long reach of time. We treasure the delight of living! Born for some beautiful purpose, we grow into some accomplishment, and wither away into some memories. Like the flowers of the grass we all fall. Only the promises of God stand forever!

DECEMBER 1

Inasmuch as you did it to one of the least
of these My brethren, you did it to Me.
—Matthew 25:40 (NKJV)

In Other Words…

Worship is a many splendored thing that may
transpire within a sanctuary, or along our daily
walk. When we reach out to help someone in
need, we are serving the Lord; the deed becomes
an act of worship. Our actions may be public or
private, but when given with a thankful heart,
they become worship. God knows our hearts.

DECEMBER 2

Be still, and know that I am God; I will be exalted among the nations, I will be exalted in the earth.
—Psalm 46:10 (NKJV)

In Other Words...

We are unnerved, by confounding situations beyond our understanding. We feel challenged by truths that unsettle our hearts and minds, causing immeasurable pain and discomfort. We know the things of God are the things of God; His Holy Spirit will unravel our confusion at the proper time. Let us be still, and know that God will help us, just as He promised.

DECEMBER 3

And this is life eternal, that they might know You, the only true God, and Jesus Christ whom You have sent.
—John 17:3 (NKJV)

In Other Words...

May we know deep within our bones the truth that God is over all! We are each incomplete without the indwelling of His Holy Spirit. None of us is master of it all...pompous as we may presume to be! We are frail human beings in need of the Way, the Truth, and the Life that blessed trinity of God sent to us through His Only begotten Son, Jesus Christ, our Redeemer.

DECEMBER 4

For you know the grace of our Lord Jesus
Christ, that, though He was rich, yet for your
sakes He became poor, that you through
His poverty might become rich.
—2 Corinthians 8:9 (NKJV)

In Other Words…

The riches of heaven did not keep our Lord Jesus
from coming down to earth to rescue us from
our lost condition. He became poor, forsaking
everything for our sake, in order to provide
us with the opportunity to become rich with
eternal salvation by trusting in Him as the very
Son of God, and our blessed Redeemer!

DECEMBER 5

Do you not know that your body is the temple
of the Holy Spirit who is in you, whom you
have from God, and you are not your own?
For you were bought at a price; therefore
glorify God in your body and in
your spirit, which are God's.
—1 Corinthians 6:19-20 (NKJV)

In Other Words...

Consider whose we are! As children of God,
we have been created for good works, not mere
worldly pleasures. How awesome to consider
the reality that the Holy Spirit resides within
us from the moment of our redemption, when
we were adopted by faith! Our body is His holy
temple to be honored with care. May we always
be available to God for His plans to be fulfilled.

DECEMBER 6

Do all things without complaining and disputing,
that you may be blameless and harmless,
children of God without fault in the midst of
a crooked and perverse generation, among
whom you shine as lights in the world.
—Philippians 2:14-15 (NKJV)

In Other Words...

How can peace come in this world? It is a challenge
that begins with each of us. If we only brighten
the corner where we are, a glow of peace might
begin to grow! If our lives become a reflection of
the light of God's love, we might shine brightly
in this dark and quarrelsome world. If we speak
only words of peace to one another, a spark
of loving peace will surely begin to glow and
grow. May God help us to let our light shine!

DECEMBER 7

I can do all things through Christ,
who strengthens me.
—Philippians 4:13 (NKJV)

In Other Words…

God is good; He will never allow us to be challenged
beyond what He will help us to bear. His Holy
Spirit within us provides strength and endurance
far more than we could ever imagine! Breathe
deeply, be still; know that God is with us always,
through whatever comes or doesn't come.
Calmly, claim His promises!

DECEMBER 8

I have loved thee with an everlasting love.
—Jeremiah 31:3 (KJV)

In Other Words...

Everlasting is a long time. Forever, always, infinity, eternity; these are words that describe what is beyond our human ability to measure. God's love for His children is an everlasting love. We love God, because He first loved us. He loved us so much that He gave His only begotten Son to become our redeemer! God demonstrated His own love, in that while we were yet sinners, Christ died for us! By faith in Him, life everlasting becomes secured for all eternity!

DECEMBER 9

Since we are surrounded by so great a cloud of witnesses, let us lay aside every weight, and the sin which so easily ensnares us, and let us run with endurance the race that is set before us, looking unto Jesus, the author and finisher of our faith, who for the joy that was set before Him endured the cross, despising the shame, and has sat down at the right hand of the throne of God.
—Hebrews 12:1-2 (NKJV)

In Other Words...

Imagine, if we can, that surrounding us is a heavenly cloud of witnesses, a mighty cheering section of saints and angels encouraging us as we run this race of life! When we stumble and fall, they call us to get up and keep on going. We are reminded of all that Jesus endured on Calvary's shameful cross, as He bore our sins, and provided for our salvation! He is the author and finisher of our faith, by His sacrificial death and miraculous resurrection from the dead! One day our life's journey will be complete; may we thankfully strive to run the race with joy and glory for Him, by His grace!

DECEMBER 10

He which hath begun a good work in you will
complete it until the day of Jesus Christ.
—Philippians 1:6 (KJV)

In Other Words…

We children of God by adoption have a purpose in
life. There is work for us to do that will be placed
upon our hearts at some moment in time; an
epiphany of clear enlightenment, a brainstorm of an
idea! Such a special event is not to be ignored, for
the Holy Spirit is nudging us to carry out the plan
God has for us. Daily tasks may be distracting, but
we will refocus with determination, until the work
God has graciously honored us to do is complete.

DECEMBER 11

Put on the whole armor of God, that ye may be able to stand against the wiles of the devil.
—Ephesians 6:11 (KJV)

In Other Words…

Be prepared! The inspired Word of God will protect our minds and hearts from the onslaught of the world's enticing temptations. God's promises are the armor to shield our lives from sin, which only leads ultimately to our destruction! Be on guard for the surprise attack that may steal upon us when we least anticipate. We will be fortified by God's gracious wisdom and mercy!

DECEMBER 12

Be kindly affectionate one to
another…rejoicing in hope,
patient in tribulation, continuing steadfastly in prayer.
—Romans 12:10 (NKJV)

In Other Words…

As we reach out with love toward one another, may
we consider their needs high above our own. Let us
celebrate the joy that abounds among us, even as we
hope for peace to grow and become rooted deeply
within every heart. May the sorrows of mankind be
replaced with thankful gladness and faithful prayer.
Thy will be done, O Lord, on earth as it is in heaven!

DECEMBER 13

For I know the thoughts that I think toward you, says the Lord, thoughts of peace and not of evil, to give you a future and a hope.
—Jeremiah 29:11 (NKJV)

In Other Words...

How reassuring to know that You are thinking about each of us, O Lord. Your words give courage to our changeable minds, as we strive to envision what is about to happen in our lives. You know what lies ahead, and promise us peace and not evil, a future and a hope for blessings we cannot begin to imagine. We thankfully claim Your wonderful promises, O Lord, with humility and great joy!

DECEMBER 14

Now unto him that is able to do exceeding abundantly above all that we ask or think, according to the power that works in us, unto him be glory in the church by Christ Jesus throughout all ages, world without end. Amen.
—Ephesians 3:20-21 (KJV)

In Other Words…

The power of God in the lives of His children is above comprehension. Those who are meek become mighty; abundantly strong in faith to work for the glory of Christ Jesus through all generations! May honor and praise be given to Him forever and ever. Amen.

DECEMBER 15

For this is the love of God, that we
keep His commandments.
—1 John 5:3 (KJV)

In Other Words...

Obedience was carefully instilled in us as children.
For our safety and civility, loving parents trained
us to know how to cope and thrive. By their
example and patient instruction, we obediently
learned how to progress correctly with success.
Celebrations of genuine pleasure and sweet affection
ensued! We found delight in showing our love
by our obedience! Rejection of their teachings
would result only in sadness. It is the same with
our response to God. Our love for Him is shown
by our obedience to His commandments.

DECEMBER 16

Know ye that the Lord, He is God; it is He that
hath made us, and not we ourselves; we are
His people and the sheep of His pasture.
—Psalm 100:3 (KJV)

In Other Words...

A shepherd guards his flock with tender care and
caution. Sheep are easily overtaken by predators,
for they seem unaware of the dangers that exist in
the world. They are vulnerable and consistently
careless about being cautious. Just like sheep,
humanity is in need of a shepherd! The psalmist
was inspired by God to assure us that we are
blessed to have the Lord Himself as our protector,
our personal shepherd! If we will stay near to
Him, the Lord will guard, guide, and lead us
safely into pleasant pastures of abundant living.

DECEMBER 17

There is no other name under heaven given among men by which we must be saved.
—Acts 4:12 (NKJV)

In Other Words...

Great wisdom has been handed down to us through the ages. We treasure the wise counsel of our forefathers and countless sages of old. Their writings instruct and inspire our seeking minds. Far beyond the value of their scholarly advise is the Word of God! Through the sacrifice of Jesus Christ the ultimate revelation of God's love was given to us. The only begotten Son of God, Jesus Christ, is the Way, the Truth, and the Life given for our salvation! Amen.

DECEMBER 18

At the name of Jesus every knee should bow…
and that every tongue should confess that Jesus
Christ is Lord, to the glory of God the Father.
—Philippians 2:10-11 (KJV)

In Other Words…

The day will come when everyone will bow down
to confess the reality that Jesus Christ is Lord, to
the glory of God the Father. Thankfully, those who
live with faith have already done so! The Trinity
of God will be fully revealed for all mankind to
understand the majesty of the Father, Son, and
Holy Spirit. How blessed we are to trust our eternal
future to Triune God's only begotten Son, Who
provided the way to salvation by His grace! Gladly
we bow and adore Jesus Christ, our Redeemer!

DECEMBER 19

In Him we have redemption through
His blood, the forgiveness of sins,
according to the riches of His grace.
—Ephesians 1:7 (NKJV)

In Other Words…

To grasp the fact that Jesus came to rescue mankind
from the final reward of sin is beyond goodness
and mercy! It is incredible love beyond measure!
Jesus sacrificed His divine perfection to bear
the burden of our sins on Calvary's cruel cross.
He came to earth for that purpose! Jesus Christ
became the ultimate unblemished sacrifice for
the redemption of each and every believer. It is
by His marvelous grace that we can be saved!

DECEMBER 20

There is no fear in love; but perfect love casts out fear,
because fear involves torment.
—1 John 4:18 (NKJV)

In Other Words...

When a good work is accomplished, or attempted,
some devious impact may suddenly invade our
thinking. Doubt, fear, or torment may attack our
trust! This is how the deceiver of the world enjoys
crashing in on our faith. A confounding event, or a
medication given during a hospital stay, may cause us
to be weakened! Breathe deeply; recall the promises
of God; sing His praises softly over any confusion.
Doubt, is never given by God! Love, peace, mercy,
and grace are His marvelous gifts! Be still; know
that the comforting Holy Spirit of God casts out fear!
Know that the love of God is always victorious!

DECEMBER 21

These things I have spoken unto you, that
in Me you may have peace. In the world
you shall have tribulation; but be of good
cheer; I have overcome the world.
—John 16:33 (NKJV)

In Other Words...

Thank you for the gracious promises You have
given to Your children! Your promises heap
blessings upon our hearts, O Lord! You are our
mighty encourager! Your Holy Word overflows
with good cheer, filling our souls with peace. Your
promises replace our fears with courage and faith
in Your loving kindness. Tribulation may abound,
but You have overcome the world! May Your will
be done on earth, Lord, just as it is in heaven.

DECEMBER 22

A man's heart plans his way, but
the Lord directs his steps.
—Proverbs 16:9 (NKJV)

In Other Words...

We dream and scheme about many things; it is
part of our human condition. Before acting on
any impulsive considerations, we would be wise
to compare our ideas with the advise of God's
Holy Word. The Lord directs His children onto
paths of righteousness, never onto damaging
pitfalls. Trusting God obediently, may we follow
His directions for our good, and for His glory!

DECEMBER 23

The Lord shall preserve thy going out and thy coming
in from this time forth, and even forevermore.
—Psalm 121:8 (KJV)

In Other Words…

Stay close beside me, O Lord, I pray. I know safety
only when Your Holy Spirit comforts me with Your
nearness. You promised to be with Your children
always, even to the end of the age! Why do I fail
to remember that blessing? Why do I flounder
about here and there? May my faith increase,
Lord! May I celebrate Your nearness, wherever
I may be, at all times! How good to know the
peace of Your loving care surrounding me!

DECEMBER 24

For I know whom I have believed, and
am persuaded that He is able to keep that
which I have committed unto Him
until that day.
—2 Timothy 1:12 (KJV)

In Other Words...

The Holy Bible is true; it is the inspired Word of
God. Loving communication with mankind began
with the splendor of God's creation of the universe.
The Holy Bible tells of the majesty of God's loving
intervention by grace to mankind throughout
the ages. God personally communicated His love
through His only begotten Son, Jesus, who came
down from heaven to earth to provide redemption
for all mankind. The Holy Spirit of God convicts of
sin and the need for salvation through the loving
sacrifice, death, and resurrection of Jesus Christ.
Eternal life begins with faith in the trinity of
God the Father, God the Son, God the Holy Spirit!
The Bible tells me so.

DECEMBER 25

Return to your own house, and tell what
great things God has done for you.
—Luke 8:39 (NKJV)

In Other Words…

As we gather together, may we remember to tell
about the loving blessings God has so kindly given
to each of us. We carefully choose nice gifts for
our dear ones, just as God lovingly heaps His good
gifts upon us. Christmas is a time for reflection
and gratitude, when the thankfulness of our hearts
may be expressed for all to hear. God has given us
everything good that exists; even coming down to
earth and giving Himself for our salvation! There
is joy in witnessing a child's delight over each gift,
and hearing their sweet words of appreciation.
May we bless God with truly thankful hearts,
as we celebrate the joys surrounding all of us at
Christmas time!

DECEMBER 26

The Lord is near to those who have a broken
heart, and saves such as have a contrite spirit.
—Psalm 34:18-19 (NKJV)

In Other Words...

To feel despondent is something we have all
experienced at one time or another. Feeling sad,
or broken hearted, can lead us to depression or
despair. Our Lord is all knowing; He understands
the moods we go through better than we are able to
comprehend. The comforting strength of the Holy
Spirit saves us, as we yield to His power within us.
The strength of the Lord is made perfect in
our weakness! Breathe deeply, patiently rest,
as His blessed healing begins and becomes
sustained for our good, and for His glory.

DECEMBER 27

We should no longer be children, tossed to an fro and carried about with every wind of doctrine, by the trickery of men, in the cunning craftiness of deceitful plotting, but, speaking the truth in love, grow up in all things unto Him who is the head...Christ.
—Ephesians 4:14-15 (NKJV)

In Other Words...

It is time to take stock of things! Let's itemize what we value most: our beliefs that remain firm and inviolable, the people we love and treasure beyond measure, God's merciful gift of abundant provision throughout all time. May we determine to discard those crafty ideas or distractions that fritter away our attention daily, deceiving us with cunning trickery and lies. We need to speak the truth in love to our focused mind and grow up in all things! May we choose to honor the life God planned for each of His children, beginning today!

DECEMBER 28

Most assuredly, I say unto you, he that hears
My word, and believes in Him who sent Me
has everlasting life, and shall not come into
judgment, but has passed from death unto life.
—John 5:24 (NKJV)

In Other Words...

Proclaim this blessed promise for all
generations to hear: Jesus assures everyone
that He has provided for our
salvation! Hear His word; believe in Him! Know
that He is the only begotten Son of God, sent
from heaven to earth for the redemption of
mankind! We may not be able to comprehend
such abundant grace, yet by faith in the word of
God we become the adopted children of God!
Jesus offers His promise of merciful forgiveness,
everlasting life, no judgment, and eternity in
heaven! Praise God from Whom all blessings flow!

DECEMBER 29

Grace and peace be multiplied unto you through the
knowledge of God, and of Jesus our Lord.
—2 Peter 1:2 (KJV)

In Other Words...

The more we study the promises of God's Holy
Word, the more knowledgeable we become. We
grow in our personal relationship with our Father
God, and with His only begotten Son, Jesus, our
Lord and Savior. The Holy Spirit of God gently
leads us in understanding the will of God for each
of His children. Grace and peace are multiplied,
as we are transformed by enlightenment!

DECEMBER 30

Now unto him that is able to keep you from falling, and to present you faultless before the presence of his glory with exceeding joy, to the only wise God our Savior, be glory and majesty, dominion and powers, both now and forever. Amen.
—Jude 1:24-25 (KJV)

In Other Words…

Let us humbly bow down in gratitude to God our Savior, who protects and guides us throughout life's earthly journey, and beyond, into His glorious presence within the splendor of heaven's eternity. With exceeding joy for His glorious wisdom, majesty, and dominion over all, we thankfully praise the blessed trinity of God both now and forever. Amen.

DECEMBER 31

Let those also who love Your name be joyful in
You, for You, O Lord, will bless the righteous; with
favor You will surround him as with a shield.
—Psalm 5:11-12 (NKJV)

In Other Words...

This day is a time for celebration! Let all the children
of God be joyful in their love of You, O Lord, for
You have blessed the righteous with special favor,
surrounding them with your merciful protection.
Praise God from Whom all blessings flow! Amen.

Printed in the United States
By Bookmasters